Women and Poetry

POETS ON POETRY

DAVID LEHMAN, GENERAL EDITOR

Allen Grossman *The Long Schoolroom*
Jonathan Holden
  Guns and Boyhood in America
Andrew Hudgins *The Glass Anvil*
Carol Muske *Women and Poetry*

A. R. Ammons *Set in Motion*
Douglas Crase *AMERIFIL.TXT*
Suzanne Gardinier
  A World That Will Hold All the People
Kenneth Koch *The Art of Poetry*

DONALD HALL, FOUNDING EDITOR

Martin Lammon, Editor
  Written in Water, Written in Stone
Philip Booth *Trying to Say It*
Joy Harjo *The Spiral of Memory*
Richard Tillinghast
  Robert Lowell's Life and Work
Marianne Boruch *Poetry's Old Air*
Alan Williamson *Eloquence and Mere Life*
Mary Kinzie *The Judge Is Fury*
Thom Gunn *Shelf Life*
Robert Creeley *Tales Out of School*
Fred Chappell *Plow Naked*
Gregory Orr *Richer Entanglements*
Daniel Hoffman *Words to Create a World*
David Lehman *The Line Forms Here*
  · *The Big Question*
Jane Miller *Working Time*
Amy Clampitt *Predecessors, Et Cetera*
Peter Davison
  One of the Dangerous Trades
William Meredith
  Poems Are Hard to Read
Tom Clark *The Poetry Beat*
William Matthews *Curiosities*
Charles Wright *Halflife* · *Quarter Notes*
Weldon Kees
  Reviews and Essays, 1936–55
Tess Gallagher *A Concert of Tenses*
Charles Simic *The Uncertain Certainty*
  · *Wonderful Words, Silent Truth*
  · *The Unemployed Fortune-Teller*
Anne Sexton *No Evil Star*
John Frederick Nims *A Local Habitation*

Donald Justice *Platonic Scripts*
Robert Hayden *Collected Prose*
Hayden Carruth *Effluences from the*
  Sacred Caves · *Suicides and Jazzers*
John Logan *A Ballet for the Ear*
Alicia Ostriker
  Writing Like a Woman
Marvin Bell *Old Snow Just Melting*
James Wright *Collected Prose*
Marge Piercy
  Parti-Colored Blocks for a Quilt
John Haines *Living Off the Country*
Philip Levine *Don't Ask*
Louis Simpson *A Company of Poets*
  · *The Character of the Poet*
  · *Ships Going into the Blue*
Richard Kostelanetz
  The Old Poetries and the New
David Ignatow *Open Between Us*
Robert Francis *Pot Shots at Poetry*
Robert Bly *Talking All Morning*
Diane Wakoski *Toward a New Poetry*
Maxine Kumin *To Make a Prairie*
Donald Davie *Trying to Explain*
William Stafford
  Writing the Australian Crawl ·
  You Must Revise Your Life
Galway Kinnell
  Walking Down the Stairs
Donald Hall *Goatfoot Milktongue*
  Twinbird · *The Weather for Poetry* ·
  Poetry and Ambition · *Death to the*
  Death of Poetry

Carol Muske

Women and Poetry

TRUTH, AUTOBIOGRAPHY, AND THE SHAPE OF THE SELF

Ann Arbor

THE UNIVERSITY OF MICHIGAN PRESS

Thanks to David Lehman for clear and insightful editorial advice
and friendly encouragement and moral support. Thanks also to my
husband David Dukes for general organizational assistance,
including hours of photocopying, stapling, and ordering essays and
reviews. And finally to Michelle Latiolais, natural-born writer, critic,
and friend extraordinaire: *merci toujours, ma cherie.*

2000   1999   1998   1997   4   3   2   1

A CIP catalog record for this book is available from the British Library.

Library of Congress Cataloging-in-Publication Data

Muske, Carol, 1945–
     Women and poetry : truth, autobiography, and the shape of the
self / Carol Muske.
          p.   cm. — (Poets on poetry)
     ISBN 0-472-09624-9 (cloth). — ISBN 0-472-06624-2 (paperback)
     1. American poetry—Women authors—History and criticism.
     2. Women and literature—United States—History—20th century.
     3. American poetry—20th century—History and criticism.
     4. Autobiography—Women authors.   5. Self in literature.   I. Title.
     II. Series.
     PS151.M85   1997
     811.009'9287—dc21   97-6446
                                                                         CIP

Contents

Women and Poetry: Some Notes

The *and* in "Women and Poetry" appears to maintain a respectful distance between two protectorates. When we move the terms in tighter, next to each other, the words get nervous. *Women* becomes a qualifier, and *poetry* cringes—what *is* a *woman poet?*

Woman poet—on the face of it, the term might appear condescending. Nevertheless, it came to exist in the 1960s and 1970s as less a descriptive than an unconscious prescriptive: the distinction made between one version of history and another. The prototypical *woman poets* of the twentieth century are, of course, Sylvia Plath and Adrienne Rich. Their poems seem inevitably framed in that context. It is hard to read their early work without experiencing it as *anticipatory;* we know what is to come; we know that each poet is going to have it out with history, as Rich has written of Dickinson, "on her own premises."

They were (along with Anne Sexton) the beginning of an era. Prior to this era the categories were set well apart. *Women* and *poets*. Of course, there was the Uber-frau-ish "poetess," a dread diminutive with an arched eyebrow over every syllable. *Woman poet* was used, but with about the same degree of gravity as *poetess*. But there were always women who wrote poetry. Some were major voices; some were not. There were also wives, mistresses, girlfriends, and secretaries—muses. Sometimes women poets got mixed up with the rest. How could one tell them apart?

There used to be a "black book" certain male poets would share with one another before out-of-town readings. Names and

---

A version of this essay originally appeared in *Michigan Quarterly Review* 35, no. 4 (fall 1996): 586–607, special issue "The Poets Voice."

phone numbers of young ladies in Poughkeepsie or Duluth who were guaranteed (by previous trial and documented experimentation) to be impressed enough by a bit of offhand enjambment to morph into pulsing dithyrambs and cheerfully succumb. What if one of these black book entries wrote poetry? How would she be classified? A red-hot footnote, or poetess, or both?

The distinction "woman poet" was meant to do more than provide an instant rejoinder-replacement to two polite epithets: poetess and phone-book muse. It was meant to *bear witness* to a truth. It was meant to complement Muriel Rukeyser's famous lines: "What would happen if one woman told the truth about her life? The world would split open." We are then bound to ask: *what* truth? These words also split the world of poetry written by women in two: those whose "self" stood as representative of various truth and those who continued to write as if the self was a fiction.

The aforementioned black book summed up the sexual politics of the 1950s: cocktails and hushed conversation after the reading and all the little poetesses in a row; a discreet phone number for later in the evening—a world that was orderly, predictable. But soon, that world did split open.

That world, split and presplit, is unintentionally documented by Carolyn Kizer, editor of *One Hundred Great Poems by Women,* who took pains (as she makes clear in her introduction to the book) not to include any poems by women about "romance or domesticity"—*thereby remaining conventional cultural expectations as to subject matters*—or the "conditioned truths" of women's lives.

These deliberate exclusions produce an unintentional "scientific" literary study (a control group) on women poets and subject matter. If "romance" and "domesticity"—the traditional preoccupations of women of all ages—are precluded, what is it that women then write about?

From the earliest poems onward, the poets wonder about the "self," a woman's self, defined as it often is as *other.* In what is believed to be Anne Boleyn's poem (perhaps a rejoinder to Thomas Wyatt, whose famous poem "Whoso List to Hunt" marks her as a "possession" of the king's), the author cries out: "Say what ye list, it will not be; / Ye seek for that can not be found."

Next is the mercurial, bardic Queen Elizabeth I:

> I am, and not; I freeze and yet am burned;
> Since from myself, my otherself I turned!
>> "Self and the Otherself"

The question of *self,* for a woman poet (not to mention a *queen's* problems in this regard) is continually vexing. The anthology bears witness to this "dislocation" of self through five centuries of poetry by women. It is a complaint unfamiliar to us historically, duly acquainted as we are with the forebearance of the Madonna, likewise the talking whore or sybil, as well as the voice that sings beyond the genius of the sea.

Kizer has eschewed any restrictions on the voice of the "other," including the restriction of *approved* subjects. What she has presented here is a distinct, separate expression of self within a chronological selection of women's poetry and a loneliness within the self unrelated to longing for others, a psyche unsplit by "love" ("If just one woman told the truth about her life . . ."). "Let Greeks be Greek and women what they are," cries the worthy Anne Bradstreet. And what *is* a woman's self? When ancient "Ephelia" cries, for example, "My soul is Masculine," it does not seem to me that she wishes to be male, rather that she wishes mightily to express the soul of Ephelia.

Again and again this sentiment appears as longing for the validation of a past, a tradition. And, not surprisingly, the voice is often wounded or angry. Witness Anne Killigrew, a seventeenth-century poet, in her poem "Upon the Saying That My Verses Were Made by Another":

> The envious age, only to me alone,
> Will not allow what I do write, my own;
> But let them rage, and 'gainst a maid conspire,
> so deathless numbers from my tunefull lyre
> Do ever flow . . . I willingly accept Cassandra's fate
> To speak the truth, although believed too late.

These poets were, of course, almost without exception members of the upper classes, titled dames whose servants provided the time necessary for writing. Later, says Kizer, when the aristocratic ladies gave up on literature, or gave up on circulating it, writing was taken over by "spinsters, who predominate, from the Brontës right down to Marianne Moore." We hear Emily Dickinson aptly inquire, "I'm nobody, who are you?"

Poetess, muse, spinster; tinker, tailor, spy—one notices the difference in emphasis. It appears that to write freely one needs relief from exacting circumstance—one needs independence and an understanding of what exactly *silence* implies. One might infer, then, that in order to write poetry a woman needs an *unmarried* self, a "spinster" self (besides a room of one's own and a little sugar bowl).

Ann Killigrew's longing to "speak the truth" is echoed through the centuries—though this longing is altogether distinct from the "truth and honor" code of men. The inclination to *bear witness* seems aligned with the missing self. By the time we arrive at Adrienne Rich and Sylvia Plath, the woman poet's tradition remains no tradition. All those isolated particles of truth, from Aphra Behn to Emily Dickinson to H. D., have become a wave of probability.

The desire for a historical self and the desire for a "truth-telling self," or "real self," merge into a single drama, or a single dramatic voice. In Rich's case the dramatic personae that began to fill her pages seemed (especially to young poets like me, reading her avidly) irrefutably, necessarily, *her*. All the way from "The Tourist and the Town" in *The Diamond Cutters* to the Wild Child, from the mermaid in *Diving into the Wreck* to Elvira Shateyeva, Marie Curie, or Caroline Herschel, it was Adrienne Rich, now a fearless and furious repudiation of the polite coed (who'd sweetly intoned in *A Change of World:* "Neither with rancor at the past / Nor to upbraid the coming time"), whose call to arms reconstituted the female literary "self." Some male critics reviled her in intemperate prose, while women read her passionately, changing their lives on a line from one of her poems. I can vouch for it: the voice speaking from her poems changed me, and gave me courage as a young poet.

When I arrived in New York City in 1971 I joined consciousness-raising groups, but I found it impossible to express my own sense of conflict. I eventually sought out women in prison, because their isolation and extremity reflected a dislocation I felt in my own life and writing. To anyone who would listen, I said that I believed that a civilization was judged by the way it treated its most helpless citizens, those in its institutional care—inmates of prisons and mental hospitals, in particular, women. But it was also true that I wanted to be an *outlaw,* bold and uncompromised, not the split being that I seemed to myself. I felt like a fake to myself: a feminist and would-be political activist who was too drawn to the literati, ambitious cutthroat editors, glitzy dinner parties. I met literary friends, late at night, down in the Village. Confused, I separated from my then-husband, an activist-doctor, a wonderful man. I felt that I had no self and I thought that I lived in two irreconciliable worlds, politics and poetry. I longed to see the two come together.

It struck me that the women in prison were living lives capable of providing instruction, and I went into the prisons without knowing exactly what that meant. I set up a writing program for inmates at the Women's House of Detention on Riker's Island then expanded the program (called Art without Walls, née Free Space) to other prisons, recruited writer friends, and began to teach writing workshops. I fervently wished that from this most "silent" population, strong voices would emerge. I was twenty-five or twenty-six years old, too young to understand the source of my own sense of women as "outlaws," my romantic regard for women who loved outside the law: family, church, politics. I felt that women were natural anarchists, so I frequented a setting in which, I hoped, all abstractions about women and their behavior would become passionately, relievedly, literal. I would encounter women whose lives had been acts of defiance, women who were unafraid. In my passion for extremity I wanted the poem itself to change.

> . . . two women, eye to eye
> measuring each other's spirit, each other's
> limitless desire,
>> a whole new poetry beginning here.
>> "Transcendental Etude"

There was a breakthrough that thrilled me: the humble job of editing a poem began to reflect the emergence of female identity. Rich comments on "The Tourist and the Town," a poem from *The Diamond Cutters:*

> The pronouns in the third part of the poem were originally masculine. But the tourist was a woman, myself, and I never saw her as anything else. In 1953, when the poem was written, some notion of "universality" prevailed which made the feminine pronoun suspect, "personal." In this poem . . . . I have altered the pronouns not simply as a matter of fact but because they alter, for me, the dimensions of the poem.

An act as small yet symbolic as altering the pronouns in a poem restored it to that "other universality," the unrecognized referent: She. A She who was also an "I." The self in women's poetry, by that altered pronoun, had become immediate *and* historical. And, unlike previous centuries, its immediacy and historicism rose from ordinary women.

Yet there was a futuristic feel to this She as well. Nothing seemed to be separating who she was from a *new* past and a future—no more spinsters and spies.

Well,
She's long about her coming, who must be
more merciless to herself than history.
Her mind full to the wind, I see her plunge
breasted and glancing through the currents,
taking the light upon her
at least as beautiful as any boy
or helicopter.

("Snapshots of a Daughter-in-law")

That bionic image was, of course, inspired by Simone de Beauvoir's woman of a new age: "she is a helicopter and she is a bird." Rich's readers could feel her evolving self in struggle, "long about her coming," pushing out through the domestic toward some wild future ideal.

The She of *Ariel,* on the other hand—fiery, dark, death obsessed, explosively self-destructive—was conflated with Plath's personal desperation. This was an alternative vision of a future that liberated the suffering consciousness from its painful constraints but destroyed the physical self in the process. Plath captured the collective imagination with her challenge to an unjust past. Rich also summoned history and held it to account but, simultaneously, beamed it forward in time. At that moment, Rich offered the possibility of turning, transformed, from the ruins of the past and, in true 1960s and post-Wordsworthian style, dreamed of a common language, a relocation of feminism, outside the "phallo-centered, written-out" vulgate. Outside the "center." Plath's vision (or the vision of *Ariel*) occurred at the bloody intersection of the personal and historical—and Plath, like a well-trained terrorist, blew herself up with the corrupt installation.

So, we have the two stances:

> I am bombarded yet   I stand
> I have been standing all my life in the
> direct path of a battery of signals
> the most accurately-transmitted most
> untranslatable language in the universe
>
> (Rich, "Planetarium")

> And I
> Am the arrow
> The dew that flies
> Suicidal, at one with the drive
> into the red
>
> Eye, the cauldron of morning.
>
> (Plath, "Ariel")

What did these passages convey to a young woman poet? Two statements; two shapes of longing—one shape projecting its own arc like a missile and the second a tower, Mrs. Ramsay's lighthouse beacon, the longed-for horizon, unflinching. The two positions appealed to me. Rich's stood for bold, unintimidated word power, courage of conviction; Plath's for fearless harrowing insight, Houdini-like escapes from the conventional idiom. More significantly, both poets gave speech to women's silence—and Rich's language embodied women's power to *act*, women's new and unintimidated anger, and (though this can only be glimpsed over time, and I couldn't see it then) her language also revealed a fierce uncompromising Shelleyean spirit, ultimately capable of renewal, forgiveness. Plath turned feelings of personal impotence into inverse power, destructive ecstasy, and she possessed, by nature, a manner of expression that, while infinitely transcendent, kept a grim eyeball on the transgressor. Plath was a virtuoso debt collector. Neither poet seemed to be at peace with Keats' notion of negative capability (or a poet's lack of self) though this "lack of self" is precisely what gives Plath's work its tension and Rich's its politics. Plath's eye roves over objects in the landscape, filling them with her fierce disembodied will. Rich rarely extols female qualities like empathy, tender-heartedness, etc., perhaps because it happens that women may be just *too good at* negative capability, if we understand it as a kind of cultivated self-absence.

I rehearsed these two shapes, admiring, in my imagination, and catalogued them as emergent "selves" (as if there were only two choices available to the developing poetic identity: defiant resistance of lyric emotional meltdown). Apart from the compelling poetry, the implacability of each shape (syntactically and politically and, yes, as a conventional "masculine" shape now relimned) revealed something wonderful and ominous about the future. But, then, I had always been seduced by an idea of "fate" in poetry, as in life.

I watched Rich stand firm, weathering the assault of criticism, Plath ejecting from the poem's argument like a pilot from a cockpit, catapulting headlong into her own explosion—and I was edified; I burrowed in my journal and found a couple of "prophecies" I now saw fulfilled:

> Yet I am now and then haunted by some semi-mystic very profound life of a woman, which shall all be told on one occasion; and time shall be utterly obliterated; future shall somehow blossom out of the past.
>
> (Virginia Woolf)

> Someday there will be girls and women whose name will no longer signify merely an opposite of masculine, but something in itself, something that makes one think, not of any complement and limit, but only of life and existence: the feminine human being.
>
> (Rainer Maria Rilke)

Certainly, Ted Hughes understood what was in the air, the emerging shapes of longing—he understood they were *projections*—and he knew what to say about this:

> A real self, as we know, is a rare thing. The direct speech of a real self is rarer still. . . . When a real self finds language, and manages to speak, it is surely a dazzling event—as *Ariel* was.

But *Ariel*'s self, it turned out, its direct speech, was to significant degree an invention of editing. Hughes changed Plath's original manuscript order (by adding and dropping poems, altering sequence, thereby reinforcing certain themes) so dramatically that what remains of *Ariel* is a riveting, aggressive work: a suicide note to the world. As the critic Marjorie Perloff has previously established, this was not the book Plath had intended to publish. Melinda Patton, a graduate student at the University of Southern California, recently described Plath's original order as an "epic journey." She calls Hughes's reassembling of the book an "unauthorized autobiography," the conclusion that Hughes's editing argues for is the inevitability of Plath's death. The last line of the book is "Fixed stars govern a life." Plath's own version ended with the visionary "bee" poems, and the last line of her book would have read "The bees are flying. They taste the Spring." Whether her version is more life affirming is hardly the point. The point is that Plath and her suicide persona became one. Clearly, she herself chose to end her life. But did she intend that her book (a book she dedicated to her children) be read as evidence of self-destruction? We will not know. The "Russian roulette-playing" Plath (with, as Lowell had it, "six cartridges in the cylinder"), that reckless "self" cheering for its own annihilation, the desparado we all rode behind, sprang fully-armed from the head of Ted Hughes.

In her momentous essay, "When We Dead Awaken," Rich refuses the "traditional" view of the imagination (or male appropriation of its contexts) in a chilling indictment: "to be a female human being, trying to fulfill female functions in a traditional way, is in direct conflict with the subversive function of the imagination." Ironically, Hughes saw this too. Long before, Auden had complimented Rich and the poems in *A*

Change of World for their "detachment from the self and its emotions." Now it seemed the self of a woman poet could be created by sheer force of will, as Hughes created the persona of *Ariel,* editing carefully "to" the myth of the scorned woman's fury, the scorched earth of her self-destructive power. And the *idea* of an unvarying self-truth, once a psychological fiction, became an unassailable tenet of a redeemable, demonstrable past. *Thus women poets did not go back to discover a historical self, but went forward to create a self.*

I was in grade school in 1958, the year Plath and Rich met for the first time, on a rainy night at Radcliffe, after a Ted Hughes reading. I didn't encounter Plath until I was in graduate school in San Francisco in 1969. I remember my poetry teacher, Kathleen Fraser, reading "Daddy" aloud—and the effect of those brutal hypnotic epithets, incantatory but explosive: a poem of flung grenades. Who *was* this woman? Where did she get the nerve to write like that? The late afternoon sun streaming through the window lit up Kathleen Fraser's waist-length auburn hair as she sat on a high stool in front of the classroom reading the poems. She looked (I remember) luminous, backlit, as the harsh syllables fell from her lips.

The *Ariel* poems—I didn't just read them; I breathed them in; they ran in my blood. I was a timid, uncertain poet, a girl bruised in the way young women in their early twenties, trying to live independently, are inevitably bruised by circumstance. They have discovered that the world is not exactly welcoming them into its "pre-race" paddock, into the fraternal chambers in which the networks get woven, political contacts settled on a handshake.

A violent chord reverberated within me. If women needed to be *outlaws* of poetry, Plath and Rich filled the bill. If Plath was a literary Jeanne d'Arc, riding headstrong, burning, whipping her mount, straight into the jaws of death, then Adrienne Rich was Antigone, an authority above conventional law. Her famous line about Marie Curie, that "her wounds come from the same source as her power," continues to thrill me in its stark rightness. I was grateful to her, I am still grateful, that she had the courage to stand up to Creon, to hurl his words back at him. I have never found her excessive. Rather, her outspoken voice told me that women were finally free to break the taboos against writing explicitly about whatever had been hidden, glossed over, buried in shame. Still, I saw her "self" as mythological, heroic, unattainable.

All of this was, in a sense, preparatory. There was a new shape of expression emerging. I recall that Rich was widely attacked by critics for a poem called "Rape" (1972), in which she illustrated (like a police artist sketching a suspect) the claustrophobic all-surrounding sense of threat felt by a raped woman giving testimony in a police precinct about her ordeal; giving language, in the process, to women's darkest suspicion of male "authority" ("There is a cop who is both prowler and father . . ."). This poem was taken by many to be an act of linguistic violence against men, a case of reverse sexism, when Rich's intent was expository, the revelation of the consciousness of a typical woman, post–sexual trauma. Statistics bear out Rich's portrait of female distrust, yet this illustration was thought of as hyperbolic, malicious, exaggerated.

Rich reconfirmed the divisions in male and female assumptions about a shared reality; her revelations moved women to insight, anger, and the will to change. Yet what gradually emerged after the collective "internalization" of poems like "Rape," was a model, a shape of poetic discourse based roughly on *the act of testimony.*

In the evolution of this model, a voice testifying to mistreatment, for example, could offer itself as substitution *in itself* for imaginative knowledge in a poem. This poetic approach quickly became popular as a kind of verbal emergency, the post-trauma voice repeating its harrowing experience as for a transcript. Rich's poem can be taken as an unconscious precursor of what was to come stylistically: the enactment of the voice of extremity—not simply as a literary convention, rather as a *moral event.* Whereas Rich wished to demonstrate a sensibility, the poems that followed wished to *be* that sensibility.

That a poem evolves from a popular consciousness has no special significance in and of itself; it happens all the time. Nevertheless, though it is commonplace to suggest that the attractions of unadorned exhortative speech are many, it is only criticism, in its applications, that provides the architecture of the *interpretation* of that consciousness. (In this sense, criticism is like a funhouse mirror, reflecting and distorting at once.) Thus, a "second wave," which was a combined force of expressive and critical solidarity, hit the long expanse of shore covered with the footprints of Plath and Rich.

Jeredith Merrin, in her important book *An Enabling Humility,* hints at how this reinterpretation of Plath and Rich's expansiveness occurred. Examining *Stealing the Language* by Alicia Ostriker, Merrin points out how the critic fails to explore the range and various array (the "humaness") of women poets at hand, choosing rather to explicate poetry that "most often takes as its subjects the female body, female anger and violence, female eroticism." It is, she says, "writing that adopts as a conscious strategy what Ostriker, *echoing Rich,* calls 'revisionist mythmaking' and that aggressively engages the reader's attention, tends toward the colloquial and employs the autobiographical 'I' "(my emphasis). In effect, Hughes's "real self." The "real self" and the myth have now become one. The "truth" is being told—and the world is splitting open. Sort of.

Eavan Boland, the Irish poet and essayist, was eighteen (just a year older than I) and a student at Trinity College the winter that Sylvia Plath killed herself at her flat in Fitzroy Road in London in 1963. Boland remembers the cold, the "frost smoking" on the windowsill of her garden flat. When she thinks of Plath she thinks of her along with two babies under three, and she remembers the quality of that cold.

Eavan Boland also believes that women need to reconnect to a past, inhabit a self, but first she asks that some rethinking be done. She has even "created a tradition"—if we read her poem "The Journey" as a Genesis vision. Certainly, it is a "revision" of Aeneas' visit to the Underworld in the sixth book of the *Aeniad.* In the poem Sappho establishes a kind of matrilinear "line" of women poets, through Boland.

> there are not many of us; you are dear
>
> and stand beside me as my own daughter.
> I have brought you here so you will know forever
> the silences in which are our beginnings
>
> (*Outside History,* 96)

When I read this, it seemed to me that Boland had done something that Adrienne Rich had long discussed: she had established a connection, indeed a right of "succession," to a women's past, even though the poem belied her efforts by its insistence on silence as a process of understanding. The impulse is not theoretical; Boland directs herself as a character in the poem's drama. She points to the poem's gainsaying, the poem's own subversion of Sappho's message, then lets the poem stand as its own object. It is important that the poem settle in its place "outside the story," in the margins of the Book VI, for there it begins to glow with new power.

The "legacy" of the tradition refuses to be a history or to bear witness to any "new" past. As the narrator-poet begs permission to write about the suffering souls of children who died of typhus and cholera, to wave the late twentieth-century wand of witness, Sappho cautions against misrepresenting these souls in the language of possession: "what you have seen is beyond speech, / beyond song, only not beyond love."

Like Rich, Boland wishes to investigate what we take for granted about women and poetry. She isolates the same crucial "moments" in metaphor that Rich excavates then rejects as poisoned by tradition. But whereas Rich dreams of a neo-proto-language, Boland wants to reenter the extant language, resee it, reexamine this uncentered "drama of expression." Boland attacks the problem in a poststructuralist fervor; the subject/object relationship has to be reversed, since this oppressive pattern is at the heart of the argument about women and poetry. (In this fervor she defies most poststructuralist tradition as well, since woman becomes the real subject, not an object of regard.) Further, her intent, unlike that of the deconstructionists, is not to show us that all texts subvert their author's intentions but, rather, that women poets can quite deliberately subvert the textual assumptions of the dominant tradition, reshape them or honor the inevitable silence within them. I see her efforts as an attempt to "demythologize" the voice of the post-trauma self.

For my own part, I had discovered that few women had interpreted Rich as I did, that is, as Antigone. The desert crossed by Rich was now an overpopulated frontier town loud with voices, and, whereas Rich's voice opened a new shape, these other voices often seemed to make the world smaller. Instead of naming and reimagining the familiar, the familiar constituted an ongoing grievance.

"Was there really no name for my life in poetry?" Boland demands of this overtrod terrain. In her book *Object Lessons* she sees herself caught between the "heresy of romanticism" and the "new feminist angers." For Boland subversion is an "act of rescue" versus a "strategy of possession" in language. We have had, Boland feels, enough rhetoric of *ownership*. The strength of "the expressive mind" has made feminist argument till now. The spirit in which Carolyn Kizer dismisses the "domestic" would not elicit approval from Boland, but she would understand it. What she herself prefers is a quiet coup in the world we take for granted, the "sensory world which inflected the mortality of the body." Thus, an object reclaimed—silk, pearls, a tree—would be wrested free from the "ageless, perfect" state of traditional regard and "flawed" time:

> And the object the returns to rescue,
> with her newly-made Orphic powers and
> intelligence, would be herself: a fixed
> presence in the underworld of the traditional
> poem.

(233)

The object would be herself. Boland's "act of rescue" is a technique, not a stance. It too wishes to alter the shape of longing but not by creating, as Michel Foucault says, "absences" that must be filled. Women would not remain preoccupied with *unnaming*, dismantling the "masters's narratives" (a task akin to yodelling backwards.) Boland would harken to critic Page duBois's analysis of women's position in the narrative in *Sappho Burning:*

> The study of narrative structure that has been a focus of some recent literary theory often seems incapable of thinking beyond the type of text exemplified by the Homeric epic. Female characters have been described as static, fixed entities in oral literatures, and structuralists and their heirs, the semioticians, often generalize from oral texts to describe women as objects, things

to be exchanged, markers of place both geographically and textually.

Women as objects. The object is herself. How to move this object, this self? By authenticating lives? Simply by retelling women's stories as history? This is the crucial choice, and Boland's desire to "subjectify" the object differs crucially from the calculated elevation of personal circumstantial detail. The movement in the "truth-telling" poem is finally, antitruth; it sets up a persona and a history resident in a kind of uncriticizable hot zone surrounded by a *cordon sanitaire*. Thus restricted in the present, we find it harder to set critical standards or visit the past to dispassionately examine the poetry by women that is there. Yet Boland's interpretations also struggle mightily (and not always successfully) to avoid the same collective "mythification" of the self, to avoid the same implacable acceptance of the self as documentable detail. It is finally true that diction-analysis tends toward the reductive, like biography.

A poem is an *act* (or an action); a poem is forever moving through space. To me it is a grave misrepresentation to substitute stasis for this animation. In this "inert" category sits the self-referential speaker, who does not move beyond self-acknowledgment, the subject matter limiting itself to "documentable" experience.

Paradoxically, a poem can be seen to embody a "biographical" self, when in fact it does not. Ted Hughes says that Plath's life is "devoid of circumstantial biographical detail," and he is correct. Rich's poems also lack ongoing "personal facts." Both poets project an intimacy that is largely fictional. In Plath's case Hughes speculates (somewhat disingenuously, given his editing of *Ariel*) that "that lack" has given rise to the "fantasies" of Plath's readers. Despite the transparency of his position, Hughes has unintentionally touched on a useful critical insight. To project "autobiography" is to possess the subject, to "own" it, to recruit it for a cause.

Since Wordsworth introduced the ego into poetry, we have labored to understand exactly what autobiography is and why it has such power to persuade us. It seems to me that autobiography is fiction like any other narrative. One apparently arguable difference from fiction is in the intensity of the moral discourse implicit in the stories of many lives, particularly lives of suffering. Still, the power of this discourse is in no way compromised or jeopardized by the inevitable selection process that attends all "telling"; in fact, the story is often "truer" in reordering, enhancing. On the other hand, if its power to persuade is based on the insistence on a moral tautology ("all victims are innocent and good"), it manipulates the reader and provides catharsis without understanding. The difference in Rich's "story of the self" (and Plath's for that matter) is that they are not based on parable-like narratives, and they admit that there is an extenuating world.

An excerpt from Rich's poem "From a Survivor":

> The pact that we made was the ordinary pact
> of men and women in those days
>
> I don't know who we thought we were
> that our personalities
> could resist the failures of the race
>
> ("From a Survivor")

Here, "testimony" exists to confront a world beyond the self and the drama of the self, even the world of silence—or the unanswerable. The movement in the poems is not toward self-justification (or self-enclosure) but, rather, insight, *movement out of the self*. The inescapable condition of autobiography is self-justification.

What other dangers lie in the illusion (and undeniable persuasiveness) of the truth-telling self? As Louise Glück observes, "But truth of this kind will not permit itself simply to be looked back on; it makes, when it is summoned, a kind of erosion, undermining the present with the past, substituting the shifts and approximations and variety of anecdote the immutable fixity of fate and for curiosity regarding an unfolding future, absolute knowledge of that future" (*Proofs and Theories,* Ecco Press, 1995). Again, it is time that is eroded. The assumption of this self fixes not only a history, but on the nature of anticipation and expectation. A "stasis" as literal as that which is imposed by tradition on women is imposed on the imagination.

Further, if the dominant tradition has persisted in "objectifying" women, surely the counterimpulse, that of oversubjectifying the self, is as grievous an error. When ambivalence toward the self is missing, as Glück says, the written re-creation, no matter how artful, forfeits emotional authority. When Sylvia Plath writes, in "Daddy . . . "

> I have always been scared of *you*,
> With your Luftwaffe, your gobbledygoo.
> And your neat mustache
> And your Aryan eye, bright blue.
> Panzer-man, panzer-man, O You—
>
> Not God but a swastika
> So black no sky could squeak through.
> Every woman adores a Fascist,
> The boot in the face, the brute
> Brute heart of a brute like you.

. . . we feel manipulated, but we are conscious of the intent to manipulate. In fact, this crudely expressed, childish intent is emphatically part of the pathos and persona of the poem. "Daddy" is a self-indulgent, hand-cranked catharsis, not even close, by my lights, to Plath's later visionary work.

Yet, as obvious as its effects are, they seem refined by comparison to the following—Sharon Olds's "The Takers":

> Hitler entered Paris the way my
> sister entered my room at night,
> sat astride me, squeezed me with her knees,
> held her thumbnails to the skin of my wrists and
> peed on me, knowing Mother would
> never believe my story. It was very
> silent, her dim face above me
> gleaming in the shadows, the dark gold
> smell of her urine spreading through the room, its
> heat boiling on my legs, my small
> pelvis wet.

The difference between "Daddy" and the "The Takers" is the difference between a poem and testimony. Sharon Olds is an extremely talented poet, and, like Plath's "Daddy," this does not represent her best work. The fact that it was written, however, at another moment in history than "Daddy" is obvious in every facet of its presentation. Unlike "Daddy," the poem lacks any noticeable rhythmic pattern beyond the flat conversational tone of the speaker. This is a stylistic choice, a choice that cleverly counterbalances the melodrama and shocking details of the poem's content—and its (like Plath's) uneasy appropriation of the Nazi/victim paradigm. The poem also has a "journalistic" feel; unlike Plath's poem, we are presented with a recounting of incontrovertible *facts,* as distinct from a child's nightmarish, imaginings.

How interesting, then, given the solid weight of these effects, that "Daddy" still seems the more shocking—indeed, the more intrinsically true—poem?

Jeredith Merrin reiterates that "the emphasis on female patterns of suffering and struggle tends to highlight commonality while over-looking psychological and artistic difference." Merrin quotes Jan Montefiore, who asks, in *Feminism and Poetry,* "the question which such assumption of the primacy of female experience in women's poems avoids asking": simply, "What makes a poem different from autobiography, fictionalized or otherwise?"

While "When We Dead Awaken" seems to urge women toward a purely female and self-enclosed experience, Merrin notes that Rich provides a description of "a certain freedom of mind" required for a writer, as opposed to literal-minded confinement:

> freedom to press on, to enter the currents of your thought like a glider pilot . . . if the imagination is to transcend and transform experience it has to question, to challenge, to conceive of alternatives, perhaps to the very life you are living at this moment. You have to be free to play around with the idea that day might be night, love might be hate; nothing can be too sacred for the imagination to turn into its opposite or call experimentally by another name.
>
> ("On Lies, Secrets and Silence: Selected Prose, 1966–1978")

A poem is different from autobiography and the negotiation between these differing "truths" of the self is dialectical, exhilarating, and essential. It *is* a profound act of subversion—something like Keats's "negative capability." The voice of truth, like the term *woman poet,* becomes an endlessly fluid, negotiatable contract with language. Language teaches us humility *and* anarchy, and these simultaneously.

Frank Bidart, a passionately "autobiographical" poet, addresses some of these questions in the interview that ends *In the Western Night.* The notion of the poem as action, as he points out, is Aristotelian, tragedy as the imitation of an action. "But the sense that a poem must be animated by a unifying central action—that it both 'imitates' an action and is *itself* an action—has been largely ignored by twentieth-century aesthetics." Further, he describes the poem as a "journey the *shape* of which has significance."

Bidart doesn't equivocate. "All art is artifice." Yet he quotes Frost's statement: "No tears in the writer, no tears in the reader"; we have to cry those tears to make the poem convincing. But, as any actor will confirm, those tears can come from anywhere: literal, empathetic, or invented sorrow. *The emotional authority,* the emotional truth, of those tears should be recognized as the a priori condition of the poem's action—but inseparable from the poet's need to create, to fabricate, to subvert.

He describes a wonderful experiment performed by Keats: his search for "the true voice of feeling," as distinct from "the false beauty proceeding from Art." Keats set out to put an X next to the "false beauty" passages and a double line next to the true voice of feeling. The experiment failed. Keats found that he could not separate the two. "Upon my soul 'twas imagination I cannot make the distinction—Every now & then there is a Miltonic intonation—But I cannot make the division properly."

In prison, when I encouraged my students to "tell the truth about their lives," the world (or the barred cells) did not split open. Mainly, this was because there was another kind of tradition already operating in prison: the unwritten etiquette behind bars connected to one's past. Everyone came to know what everyone else's record, or "rap sheet," contained, but no one talked openly about these things. In an environment in which no one admitted guilt and the crime was not discussed, the idea of "telling all" was novel, even slightly abhorrent. And, when they finally began, tentatively, to document biography in verse, I discovered that there was a direct relationship between gravity of offense and willingness to divulge one's history. Quite naturally, writing about how one became a shoplifter (or "booster") was a bit less painful than providing details of how a family member died at one's hand.

Then one woman, a new arrival in the workshop, broke the ice. Patricia wrote an unforgettable poem about how the prison authorities had denied her the right to attend her baby daughter's funeral. Her two-year-old girl had been hospitalized after a fall just prior to her arrest and had died during her first day in prison, the previous day. Patricia wrote a savage, bitter, uncompromising poem in classic English ballad meter that called for the reader to *witness* this injustice, this unyielding official refusal to allow a mother to hold her dead baby in her arms one last time. ("My baby lyin' in a cold steel drawer . . ."). Make no mistake, the poem's voice was extreme: she was willing to "turn the prison floor red" with "screw" (correctional officer) blood to "shoot her way to her baby's side."

Like most of the incarcerated women, Patricia was poor and black. She supported herself by whatever means were available to her. And it seems she'd been arrested as an "accessory" (in an overwhelming number of cases, as I'd recently discovered, women "offenders" were companions to men who had committed crimes of armed robbery, larceny, or breaking and entering); Patricia told us she had been at her boyfriend's side when he robbed a bar with a gun. She had been sent to prison to await sentencing, while her baby died without her. Patricia was inconsolable—and unforgiving. She read the poem aloud, weeping, then let the workshop members copy it so that it could be sent out "on the drum," passed hand to hand inside the institution.

As their teacher, did I think this intemperate? Not at all. I believed the poem was its own force. After eliciting truth from these women, how could I caution them against "publication" of truth? Though I must admit, *my* sense of any poem's persuasive power precluded its being taken seriously behind bars, where it seemed to me that daily suffering exceeded language. I was taken aback by how many women wept at these words. And, beyond that initial shock, I never expected to see such regard duplicated in the minds of the prison authorities.

Nonetheless, the desperateness of Patricia's plight moved us all, and I went personally to plead with the warden to allow her to visit her daughter's grave. The warden shook her head. On my next visit to the prison, a few days later, I discovered that Patricia had been thrown into the "Bing" (solitary confinement) for an "attempt to incite a riot." Oddly (because civilians were rarely allowed in the punitive solitary area), I was permitted to visit Patricia in her tiny bare cell, with its dungeon-like observation slit, its single ceiling bulb. I expected to find her distraught, but she was filled with energy; she'd been scratching "poems" into the wall (crisscrossed with graffiti from previous tenants) using a bent spoon. She begged me to bring her Bing contraband: paper, a pen—so that she could write more. Her eyes were bright and fierce. She told me that she'd been "freed" by this experience; she felt more powerful than she ever had before in her life. I left that cell knowing with absolute clarity what had happened. I'd told my students to write the truth. Now one of them had and had been censored, had suffered cruel and unusual punishment as a result of telling that truth. I remember thinking dazedly that poetry *did* make things happen.

I went straight to the warden's office and stood before her, demanding that Patricia be released. I told her that she had acted precipitously, that the institution would never succeed in censoring the truth. I asked her to allow me to bear "responsibility" for what had happened; I'd even be willing to go to the Bing in Patricia's place or suffer whatever penalty they deemed appropriate. If Patricia were not released, if the prison would not let me take on some of Patricia's punishment, then I would go to the press and publish an exposé of this barbarous act of repression. I remember that I said "barbarous."

The warden (a pretty, military-looking black woman in her fifties) sighed deeply, opened a desk drawer, and handed me a file. Inside the file folder were coroner's photographs of a child who had been beaten to death. She said the child was

Patricia's two-year-old daughter. The warden told me that it was the district attorney's belief that Patricia's pimp had kicked and punched the baby till she died then shoved her below the floorboards of a closet in Patricia's apartment, while Patricia stood by, an accessory. Aiding and abetting first-degree homicide was the crime with which she'd been charged. The warden said that Patricia had used the poem (and me) to try to gain sympathy for herself, to get me to plead for a furlough. Once released, the warden said, she'd have disappeared. I handed the file back to her. I couldn't bear to look any longer at the tiny shattered body.

But there was something else. Not even Patricia, she went on, realized how deeply the poem would affect the other women in prison, routinely separated from their children, some destined never to see them again. (It is important to note here that the Women's Correctional Institution on Riker's Island was a detention facility, nicknamed the Women's House of Detention, as well as a prison for sentenced inmates. A majority of the women had not been convicted of any crime; they were awaiting sentencing, unable to afford bail. At that time, in the early 1970s, it was possible and legal for a detention inmate to "fall off the calendar" and end up waiting up to two years to stand trial. Since then, the laws have been changed and a detainee must appear before a judge within an allotted time. Then, as now, a woman's children—if her relatives were unable or unfit to keep them— were routinely made wards of the state at the time of her arrest, before any court appearance. A woman might finally be judged innocent and still have lost her family.)

The "near riot" caused by Patricia's poem had been a case of women quoting the poem to one another in the halls, cell to cell, shouting out lines about "screw blood" and "offing the warden" on their way to the laundry or the kitchen. Screaming the poem at the officers, louder and louder, gathering in groups to read the poem aloud—why? Because the poem said: women have no power, the state takes your children away from you, flings them into foster homes; you may never see your children again, even at death. They'd pushed up against the bars, calling out to the violators of their maternal rights. *Give them back, motherfuckers, give them back.* The emotional authority of Patricia's voice shook the foundations of the prison with more force than the planes taking off every twelve seconds from La Guardia Airport, just yards across the bay. *Give her back, motherfucker, give her back.*

I looked at the warden. She had the unthinkable photographs in front of her. But she was indeed the state, all that my Marcuse-saturated brain had learned to distrust. Yet she had proof. Whatever the truth was, I was still responsible for Patricia's time in the Bing. And I *was* responsible; the warden agreed with me on this. But she would not release Patricia from her punitive cell. Why, I asked her, if she is guilty of standing by as someone killed her daughter, why is she still writing self-exonerating poems up there? But I knew the answer even as I asked the question. Patricia was still following my assignment—telling the truth, as she perceived it.

The warden hoped that I had learned a lesson. My "punishment" was simply that I be allowed to go on teaching poetry at the Women's House—which was, of course, intolerable. I wanted to run away and never come back. But now I had to return in a different capacity: as an "offender," whose offense was treating lives and life stories with the condescension that oversimplifies truth. Each day Patricia spent in the Bing (another three days, then she was arraigned and eventually sentenced and transferred) would be on my conscience, along with my unwitting promotion of a situation that allowed the prison to use freely its formidable, unappealable powers of censorship and punishment.

But what about my own version of this story? Certainly, I have heightened some aspects, dimmed others. Should I cry that I still see those merciless black-and-white morgue photos of that broken, bruised two-year-old body? I do not. In memory the images shift in the warden's hand. What she is showing me, as I recall, is her truth, her reason for maintaining institutional order. The child's abused body exists here only as the object of other narratives, including the state's. It has no subject. And the child's voice is silenced forever. could anyone presume to speak for her? Sappho's voice cautions from Boland's poem as we beg to witness: some things are beyond speech, beyond song, not beyond love.

I know there are many ways to view this story. I was negligent and presumptuous; that's indisputable. Some people may suspect that the warden was duplicitous, offering pictures of another inmate's child. Maybe Patricia wanted to get out to locate the pimp, to kill him. I don't know. I will never know, though later I heard from an appellate lawyer that Patricia had turned state's evidence against her codefendant, the pimp.

Emily again: "Tell all the truth / but tell it slant." I still believe both conflicting truths about that poem: that it was a fabrication yet was unassailable and accurate. To deny the importance of that poem would be to deny the significance of art, for the rhetorical power of its language moved people to tears, caused them to stand up and demand justice from their jailers. "Where are our children?" they cried. "This is a house of detention; we've not yet been convicted of a crime, and yet you rob us of our families." Patricia had unwittingly written of a bigger truth. And this is why the poem of witness *must exist*—because it is necessary to refresh moral life.

On the other hand, to accept the poem's veracity as an inherent component of its art would lead only to the "immutability," the stasis of prescription Glück describes, and to self-justification, indefensible and ultimately impossible. Patricia, perhaps guilty of her daughter's death, perhaps not, chose to tell her story. Her "real self" poem was the avenue to absolution. Instead of a woman who killed her child, she became a heroine, a courageous victim. Beneath the poem's syntax was a hidden shape of longing, that shape a mother's arms make holding a dead child—or perhaps the shape a mother's arms make holding a child dead by her own hand. It contained the perfect ratio of truth to invention. It moved its audience, and it offered the great extenuating fact of motherhood, thus "healing" Patricia. What more astonishing, transformative thing can art do? The truth of art, not the truth of truth. Patricia, I saw at last, might have been the outlaw I'd been looking for, but I couldn't face the dilemma she presented.

The warden was right. I'd learned a lesson: I would never have said it at the time, but I'd come to understand something inexorable about the way a poem could be. I saw how Patricia had erected a self on a form of desire. There is indeed "fabrication" in objects; there is fabrication implicit in the self, which is, after all, an object too. I came to believe that there is in the writerly imagination a deep ungovernable impulse to invent, fictionalize, to tell the truth, but "slant." And this desire rises from the same brave anarchical source as the truth-telling impulse. Each desire represents, of course, a passion for meaning, for an act that will bring order, a shape to experience.

Past, Present, Future

Backward into the Future

In 1970, in Moscow, I visited the Soviet Exhibition of Cultural Achievements and watched a videotape that celebrated the first woman cosmonaut, Valentina Tereshkova, not so much for her extraterrestrial exploits as for "being a real woman." As the official story went, Valentina fell in love with the male co-tenant of her space capsule as it orbited the Earth, and the two cosmonauts were married upon reentry. It occurred to me then that women were true victims of the "happy ending" syndrome, the future with no future in it. Ever since then I've been looking for better endings (and beginnings) to women's stories, but I see now that my mistake was looking within the narrative form itself. Women are just beginning to discover themselves, to write the stories. Adrienne Rich might say that women are themselves the future.

On March 21, 1977, Adrienne Rich spoke at Bedford Hills Correctional Facility for Women in Westchester County. Of the hundred-odd poets, lecturers, politicos, "ethics technicians," and others, male and female, who visited prisons throughout New York State in the program sponsored by Art without Walls, she was among the few interested in speaking directly and without condescension to her audience. She was discussing "Violence: The Heart of Maternal Darkness," a chapter of her book *Of Woman Born*. If she seemed a bit shy at first, it might have been because, in a room filled with women who had challenged the law in a variety of ways, her subject retained the power to shock. "Why do women beat or kill their children?" she asked,

---

From a review of *The Dream of a Common Language* by Adrienne Rich, in *Parnassus* (Spring–Summer 1979).

her voice gathering strength as she provided her audience with an answer that redefined the act of maternal violence. She was publicly breaking a taboo, saying the unthinkable: that it was not unnatural for a mother, especially a woman who had suffered violence against her own body and soul, to harbor hostility against her own children, to lash out at them in frustration and anger. She was not condoning this violence but investigating its sources, pursuing a line of thought that had obsessed her for a long time: what is most unspeakable at the heart of woman— and why.

Later the same year, at her suggestion, she returned to Bedford Hills and gave a reading to a group of writing students. She chose poems by women poets she admired and some of her own work and then invited the students to share their poems. Suddenly everyone had a poem. Suddenly everyone had a lot to say. At the end of the reading everyone applauded everyone else. (Several women asked Rich where they could get more books of poetry. Two days later her publisher, W. W. Norton, sent a catalogue, and the women selected the books they would most like to have. A few weeks after that books arrived by the hundreds— books of poetry, criticism, biography, painting, music, and psychology. Rich later characterized the women at Bedford Hills as among the most "aware" of any audience she had previously encountered.)

Having heard Rich read in many places and finding her an unashamedly didactic poet, I like to muse over her different uses of emphasis for the instruction of different audiences. At the YMHA she read dramatically "Phantasia for Elvira Shatayev" (from *The Dream of a Common Language*), an austere elegy in which Rich speaks through the persona of a Russian woman who led an all-woman mountain climbing team that perished on Lenin's Peak in 1974. The poem celebrates these brave women as members of an enlightened sisterhood of "explorers" and exhorts women everywhere to move into the "unfinished and the unbegun," a process in which, sequential thinking being arrested, the self floats free outside of time: forward into the past, backward into the future.

At the prison readings, by contrast, Rich stressed a commitment to women in "psychic extremity," in isolation, who, like

Madame Curie, the heroine of her poem "Power," find that their wounds come from "the same source as their power."

It seems to me that Rich was "prospecting" on both occasions, on the trail of the archetype and the new prototype. Holding up the lamp like some mother-guardian, a Ceres, she revealed the path lit in both directions—past and future. She implied that women must climb into the wound and study it, back to the source, the mother lode of pain and silence and the origins of power at that center. Then they must move "forward into the risk"—the words of a teacher-explorer urging her students to new heights. It seems that all women are connected, in her thinking, by the kind of thin tenacious cable worn by mountaineers—when one dangles over the abyss, the line holds, and each is pulled up by the other, the separate struggles merging into one effort. It is no accident, therefore, that Rich uses images of cartography and exploration throughout *Dream*.

Earlier, in an interview done in 1974, she commented on the "back and forth" flow of woman-energy and the special "historical" sense that should attend critical reading of writing by the neophyte "explorer":

Once you stop splitting inner and outer, you have to stop splitting all those other dichotomies, which I think proceed from that. Yourself-other, head-body, psyche-politics, them-us. The good society would be one in which these divisions would be broken down, and there (would be) much more flow back and forth. . . . At moments I have this little glimmer of it. When I'm in a group of women, where I have a sense of real energy flowing and of power in the best sense, not power of domination, but just access to sources—I have some sense of what it could be like.

Also, a lot of women are now writing poems out of their own experience, who have never written poetry before. What might sound like something very simplistic and propagandistic in a poem by such a woman, for *her* might represent a very radical dangerous exploration. And that's important too; I'm not about to write that off. I think that it's too easy to see that kind of poem in the context of the whole long complicated male tradition with its baroque, in-group quality and not realize that that woman might have gone on a limb and taken a risk every bit as painful as D. H. Lawrence was taking when he wrote as a man out of a consciousness that was very radical for his time and place. *One honors the risk,* maybe. And it can speak to others who are taking it.[1]

Is this meant to be, besides a pat on the back for good intentions, a call for relaxing critical standards? At first glance both would appear true, and yet I think that she is saying something much more fundamental and subversive. The goal of all this exploration is not the cultivation of "better women writers" but of women who will begin to write outside of the "law" of language, beyond the reach of male critical approval.

Thus, language itself in *Dream* appears to be "in the act of changing its meaning" (a definition Stanley Kunitz has given of poetry) within the framework of Rich's ideological time. For those who call her "radical" (often because they claim to recognize the voice of the demagogue in her recent poems) I suggest that this altered sense of time is her most radical statement. She moves compass-like through other people's "hours and weeks" to the inevitable north of the future, her point of view. More than assaulting the prevailing aesthetic, she assaults the *temporality* of that aesthetic, our chronological sense of ourselves—and it is in this deliberately woven time warp that *The Dream of a Common Language* begins.

Rich asks us to dream collectively, suspend our waking sense of time's authority, presuming all and nothing, as in a dream. As a clever veteran explorer of the unconscious, she knows this mined territory well enough to ask her readers to consider formally the dream as the single metaphoric device whose radar will guide us to "consciousness."

There is irony, albeit unintentional, in the choice of the dream as governing metaphor, for it is the oldest escape hatch in poetry, the begging-off of active volition in the awesome presence of the unconscious; and it would seem to obviate some of Rich's grandness of intention. Where the ego-organized brain gives itself over to the pulsing iconography of sleep-thinking, how can we talk abut the will to change? We are not talking,

---

1. *Adrienne Rich's Poetry,* edited by Barbara and Albert Gelpi (New York: W. W. Norton, 1975).

after all, about the common language, but about the dream of such a language, that familiar and safe old vehicle. The halo of dream is a kind of proscenium through which the reader will view the poem.

Rich seems to counter this objection by pointing again and again to the "old maps" in which the goddess watches over the shipwreck of rational intentions; these maps chart the great unexplored province of female "intuition" or the undermining of ego in woman, which has led to closer identification with the unconscious. Thus, the vocabulary of sleep and passive image making can coexist with the active resounding speech of the explorer, miner, and mapmaker. The result is a female tradition of unspoken, hypnotic, "shapening" thought represented by hands at work with needle, churn, or healing gesture and by midwifery, quilting, witchery, dreamwork.

Inside the dream, as in the poem "Transcendental Etude," she gets to work (echoing Muriel Rukeyser) isolating "the truths we are salvaging from / the splitting open of our lives." Again, our ordinary notions of time will be overcome—the truth of women's lives will surface in womb time, ocean time: "to wake from drowning / from where the ocean beat in us like an afterbirth / into this common acute particularity," by which she means a revivified language, "a whole new poetry beginning here."

Silence is revered as the old order of expression—the word-less judgment of the weak, the eloquent silence of the madonna, the sphinx, the filling womb. Rich uses images of "soundless speech,"

> as if a woman quietly walked away
> from the argument and the jargon in a room
> and sitting down in the kitchen, began turning in her lap
> bits of yarn, calico and velvet scraps,
> laying them out absently on the scrubbed boards

and out of the patchwork the poem emerges. This is the silence of a woman listening to the body for instruction, the emotional meteorology, the "afterbirth," that once vital but forgotten link between living beings.

Examining these poems, I find (avoiding somewhat the issue of Rich's politics as subject matter) the subversive tactics of her aesthetic necessary to the integrity of *Dream* and to the notion of "dreaming" a new language. These guerrilla techniques include the "out-timing" process I mentioned, which culminates in the floating, disjointed syntax of a poem like "Not Somewhere Else but Here," and, further, her countermanding of the "historical order" in poetry, the habit of viewing each poem written in the language as heir presumptive to the tradition. Her refusal to assume this legacy, the "approved past" in poetry, is under-scored by her image of women passing a seed from hand to hand: the matrilinear heritage does not seem to proceed hierar-chically, "down to us," as in patriarchy, but horizontally, *across* the ages. Virginia Woolf tried closing in on this idea once dur-ing some random theorizing in her diary: "Yet I am now and then haunted by some semi-mystic very profound life of a woman, which shall all be told on one occasion; and time shall be utterly obliterated; future shall somehow blossom out of the past."

Regarding "tradition," perhaps the aversion of many Ameri-can poets to what is called "political poetry" may be, in part, fear of an altered sense of time's passage—fear, in particular, of a future. Certainly, the desire to locate and define the past that obsesses contemporary poetry does seem predominantly male. The themes of the search for the lost father, the death of the father (heralded in the oedipal criticism of Harold Bloom), the son's rite of passage and nostalgia for the nuclear family, are all cloaked in ready-to-wear pathos.

This is why Rich has asked us to "honor the risk" of her dream exploration out of time—accompanying that expedition re-quires us to move outside of male history and tradition. If writ-ing from the "dream log" seems ingenuous, simplistic, she might argue that conventional critical standards seem irrelevant to this maiden voyage.

With critic Cheri Register's prescriptive approach in mind, which "attempts to set standards for literature that is 'good' from a feminist viewpoint," and, ironically, with the most weather-beaten notion of didactic poetry at hand, the reader will discover an appropriate methodology for "diving into" the

Dream. T. S. Eliot says the Virgil's *Georgics,* besides conveying information and giving moral instruction, is "beautiful poetry." He would have doubted that a combination of historical and cultural factors would ever again occur that might produce a work of pure and beautiful didacticism, such as *Dream* gives us.

Many of Rich's critics believe that she "changed" to a didactic stance rather suddenly, becoming political, radical, ostensibly hostile to men. She would agree that a change from her earlier verse (imitative of Frost, Auden, Lowell) took place—but would date the shift from just after *The Diamond Cutters* (1955), when she "embarked on a process that was tentative and exploratory," gradually transforming her life and her poetics and her politics into a single phenomenon. As she remarks in "Cartographies of Silence":

> If at the will of the poet the poem
> could turn into a thing
>
> . . . .
> If it could simply look you in the face
> with naked eyeballs, not letting you turn
>
> till you and I who long to make this thing
> were finally clarified together in its stare

The poem is a kind of embodiment of (ironically) all the poet cannot say in words, and its presence, real and unarticulated, in the actual poem forces "clarification." Still, we never see the imagined poem; we can only assume that it is powerful, like rumors of a common language whose words we never hear. Vague, catch-all words like *thing,* however, are used deliberately and, I think, mistakenly—as an overkill demonstration of the poverty of our ordinary descriptive range.

These are indeed the "risks" of writing the new language. Rich's personal doubts about employing this strategy must have been considerable at one time; in "The Roofwalker," a poem from an earlier book, she noted:

> I feel like them up there
> exposed, larger than life
> and due to break my neck.

Still, concern about the future is exactly what fuels her unique and powerful ambition to rewrite the archetypes in the cleansed vocabulary of passion and intimacy. In this vocabulary language would be rescued, excavated at the moment of metaphor, the moment of crossing over from the literal to the symbolic. *Dream* is written in a dialect that attempts to speak in metaphor without exceeding the limits of its own empirical truth, to use a language that, even in its symbols, will not lie.

Metaphor as dialect and dream as native land both demand that the reader be translator, that the old "stand-fors" will not hold: a mountain or a door will not equal its traditional metaphoric quotient. This is the mother tongue, in which remembering and imagining are the same thing and in which language, phenomenologically precocious and without hierarchical presumptions, is without dictatorial tenses, relying more on instinct than logic.

Rich's revolutionary concept of language is not new. Witness I. A. Richards heralding poetry as "capable of saving us" and "overcoming chaos" or Aragon wielding it as a weapon in the class war, or reread Valery's hymn to the "restoring" powers of words (as objects and gestures in themselves) to mark the precedent.

Ironically, similar perceptions about language among certain French critics and thinkers[2] (all male) led to mistrust of language's capacity to express *anything* accurately—leading to "terrorism" in literature, to the "literature of silence," to Maurice Blanchot's statement that the goal of language is "its own suppression."

Thus, a predictable and "pretty" philosophical impasse leads on one hand to a near-fatal brand of male petulance and to inspiration, a source of collective speculation or "dreaming," on the other. Rich, it seems, is aware of this difference too.

In the first section of *Dream* Rich is trying to define and exorcise evil power and to pit herself and her personae against its force; in the second she affirms woman-love in a ring of canticles touched with fiercely gentle power. These love poems

---

2. Jean Paulhan notes that words come to be regarded as betraying thought rather than conveying it and there is regret that words cannot be "things in themselves."

have a *body*, unlike the manifesto poems of the first section, which peer from a terrible brain, an unforgiving cyclopean eye. The love poems are very nearly incarnate, but entirely without lust, with an enormous aching homesickness for the "like" ("Homesick for myself, for her"); and, as the walls of taboo crumble, one caresses another's flesh, brushes another's hair in a witched, undersea light. The implication of choice reverberates: "I choose to love with all my intelligence."

Most of the poems in the first section are convincing. The "Phantasia for Elvira Shatayev" is starkly eloquent. In the poem the women climbers have perished, seeking a new sense of themselves. Their deaths signal an epic tradition for women, and Rich confers a deserved epic stature on this team of spiritual athletes, who, like fleeing vestal virgins, find Olympus a hostile but entirely appropriate arena for their public and private ambitions.

Though there is nothing "male" about the woman heroes (Curie, Shatayev) who populate this first section, what makes them seem "unfemale" at times necessitates a recognition of our own conventional expectations. They manifest a terseness, an economy of feeling, we are unaccustomed to associating with women. Here are women who go "beyond" love into the extremes of knowledge (science, exploration, anger) and scale the heights of their powers of imagination.

In this section of poems that articulate a "position" it is surprising that Rich would include a poem as flawed and poorly written as "Hunger." On first inspection it appears to be held together with the kind of rhetoric jam we usually get from High Places. Landscapes of snow and frozen wasteland haunt this book and, at times, paralyze the blood behind the words. This happens in "Hunger." What we get from the poem is a world starring suffering and terror—the same one we get from the newspapers—and nothing more. The failure in the poem is in the lack of the "common acute particularity" Rich extols earlier. This poem could have gained much from an individual narrative, a particular woman's story, rather than a fatuous insistence on the Everywoman skin.

Rich's tendency to generalize, to aggrandize the truth she spends so much time tracking, is disturbing. Not because I think that her occasional excesses are signs of weakness but because they are intentional. She occasionally does violence to the language just to prove she can. She uses such muscle flexing, oddly enough, to demonstrate the anger of the prophecy fulfilled—the image of the blowtorch, which she has used before, blasts away all the "ticky-tacky" in a stream of cleansing fire. In this mood she indulges in a brand of self-heroics that congratulates itself on the page—a real temptation for a woman in her position. She has, after all, made it clear that she is in possession of a quality few American poets are ever called upon to reveal: courage. She has had the courage to turn her back on a literary "future" that seemed established and undertake a whole new definition of the future of poetry. She has had the courage to stand up to her detractors and critics, for whom misogyny was cultural imperative, and make it stick. She has vindicated herself with *Dream,* a book in which she has at last found a "language" equal to her themes.

> But there come times—perhaps this is one of them—
> when we have to take ourselves more seriously or die;
> when we have to pull back from the incantations,
> rhythms we've moved to thoughtlessly
> and disenthrall ourselves, bestow
> ourselves to silence, or a deeper listening, cleansed
> of oratory, formulas, choruses, laments. . . .

and:

> No one who survives to speak
> new language, has avoided this:
> the cutting-away of an old force that held her
> rooted to an old ground
> the pitch of utter loneliness
> where she herself and all creation
> seem equally dispersed, weightless, her being a cry
> to which no echo comes or can ever come.

How can she turn back on her own eloquent counsel to "cleanse" herself of oratory and formula, after writing lines like these, and serve up the dead weight of these clichés?

Is death by famine worse than death by suicide,
than a life of famine and suicide, if a black lesbian dies
if a white prostitute dies, if a woman genius
starves herself to feed others,
self-hatred battening on her body?

This is "showcase" anger, drumbeating, Rich playing Adrienne
Rich, Avenging Goddess, with a folksy aside to Audre Lorde (to
whom the poem "Hunger" is dedicated):

I stand convicted by all my convictions—
you, too. We shrink from touching
our power, we shrink away, we starve ourselves
and each other, we're scared shitless . . .

This, I hope, is not the new language. Fortunately, Rich rarely
gives into the temptations of "oratory and formula." She is se-
cure enough now in her pioneer role to ease up her spear-
rattling vocabulary and insistence on the triumph of a collective
will that is female, outlaw, and quasimilitaristic.

The silent community of women, whom she presumably
speaks to and for, finally amounts to background, "landscape"—
thawing and vaguely ominous—for the poet's private visionary
struggle. The book ends and begins the "musing of a mind one
with her body."

What emerges, for me, despite the author's passion for order,
for a feminization of the universe that is practically Elizabethan
in concept—a "new music of the spheres"—is her loneliness.
Rich stands on an earth whose underground rivers and re-
sources symbolize for her women's past, just as the sky becomes
their future—and finds herself, finally, in between, in a state of
negative capability women know well.

In the process of attaching to men and tending children,
women have failed to know and love themselves, and it is this
division of spirit that both animates and frustrates the need for
common speech, the codification of female culture. This lan-
guage, which refuses to be tentative, suffers in its high moments
almost as much as in its lows because of the precocity of its
conclusions in a world that has yet to comprehend the problem.

Am I to go on saying
for myself, for her

This is my body,
take and destroy it?

It is an odd contradiction that the discovery of this concept of
woman language has both freed and subdued Rich. By way of
explanation I might oppose "male" and "female" thought pro-
cesses as representative of different language-making skills and
assign perfectly arbitrary characteristics to each. I might describe
the female process as associative, emotionally or instinctually
inspired, synchronous, impressionistic, producing a dreamlike
syntax; and the male process as analytic, dynamic, thematic (or
theme related), sequential, formal (as in the narrative), emotion-
ally restrained, with an externally ordered syntax.

Assuming these distinctions, Adrienne Rich would appear to
be a more male writer than say, Virginia Woolf, Louise Bogan,
Sylvia Plath, and certainly Marcel Proust. When she leans too
much on an affected, artificially sisterish tone, as in "Natural
Resources," she muffles her most individually compelling and
direct voice. At her most persuasive she is positively forensic—
fencing with imaginary analytical adversaries; her mind flying at
top speed toward a good knotty problem. In an "attitude cage,"
she is like a lioness, pacing.

The language in *Dream* is much too unfinished for us to know
what *new* and *powerful* are redefined. Ultimately, in Rich's view
all will be redefined; in the interim her explorer persona re-
mains a sort of intrepid eyewitness journalist reporting back to
News Central that a major bulletin is on the way.

I would not dream of discrediting *Dream* for its separatist
politics, and so I find its speculative aesthetic defensible, even
exciting. The few limitations I find have to do with Rich herself,
restraining herself (an ironic by-product of such unrestrained
hypothesis) and subjecting herself to penurious theming (since
the "word-as-world" is inevitably a philosophic abstraction that is
unlimited—therefore limited, even predictable and uninterest-
ing), a false "common-ness" of usage.

Sometimes this great earthquake of language is not enough

subjective, idiosyncratic ground for an imagination like Rich's. Like all poets, she still needs a little shack (a few walls, a window) in the cosmos to come home to—and from which to speak.

In the last section of *Dream,* entitled *Not Somewhere Else, but Here,* Rich is, as she says, "writing for myself." After the manifesto of the first section and the fantasy of the second, she returns to her own life, her private thoughts. Though the book sets up expectations for a "synthesis" of past and present—a leap into the future—she remains on the edge, meditating. The title poem of the section demands concentration on "the life that must be lived"; the syntax is chopped, breathless, but regular as a hurried stride through the city accompanied by murmurs of self-encouragement:

> Courage to breath   The death of October
> Spilt wine   The unbuilt house   The unmade life

The recovery of stride leads not to revelation but to a hard look at the *visionary's* business. Mourning the lost lover of the second section leads to an almost religious recognition of duty:

> Now I must write for myself   for this blind
> woman scratching the pavement   with her wand of thought
> this slippered crone inching on icy streets
> reaching into wire trash baskets   pulling out
> what was thrown away   and infinitely precious

"What was thrown away" and the grief itself are necessary for the reintegration of spirit. There is no despair in Rich. She is hard on herself, continually shaking herself awake from reveries, pointing herself back in the Right Direction. I like her in her "possessed" moods, in the trance of love or demonic speech, and in the crusader fire, burning new emblems of thought. But here, cooler now, in the most "ordinary" section of the book, I trust her humanness, her self-doubt, finally (what seems hardest for her) her love for herself.

> It seems I am still waiting
> for them to make some clear demand

> some articulate sound of gesture,
> for release to come from anywhere
> but from inside myself.
>
> ("Toward the Solstice")

The writing, too, becomes more self-possessed. "Natural Resources," a poem in fourteen parts, builds as painstakingly and succinctly as a miner's tended vein. She makes sure of her footing before each step, adjusts her light, and moves further into the poem's promise. It is another "interior monologue" poem, the mind doggedly at work on the material, wresting free chip by luminous chip the striations of revelation: "the fibers of actual life as we live it now." In bare two-line stanzas, in icepick rhythm, the poem gathers momentum and bursts like an ore-laden car from the mine shaft into light:

> My heart is moved by all I cannot save:
> so much has been destroyed
>
> I have to cast my lot with those
> who age after age, perversely,
>
> with no extraordinary power,
> reconstitute the world.

It is a natural enough ascension now to "Transcendental Etude," the most elegantly phrased and passionate soliloquy in the book. Not since Wordsworth hovered over Tintern Abbey has a poet so "appointed" landscape as symbolic grazing land. She is in the future now; she gathers nature into her visionary diction as if it existed only to serve her purposes here.

> This August evening I've been driving
> over backroads fringed with queen anne's lace
> my car startling young deer in meadows—one
> gave a hoarse intake of breath and all
> four fawns sprang after her
> into the dark maples.
> Three months from today they'll be fair game . . .
> . . . But this evening deep in summer
> the deer are still alive and free
> nibbling apples from early-laden boughs

> so weighted, so englobed
> with already yellowing fruit
> they seem eternal, Hesperidean
> in the clear-tuned, cricket-throbbing air.

The delicacy and the gentle sentiments of an earlier Rich—
the young poet enamored of the "Hesperidean" air and the
refined craft of high order—have been taken into the embrace
of the older, wiser, imperative, and more innovative voice.

> And in fact we can't live like that, we take on
> everything at once before we've even begun
> to read or mark time, we're forced to begin
> in the midst of the hardest movement,
> the one already sounding as we are born.

She is writing, as she says in "Toward the Solstice,"

> trusting to instinct
> the words would come to mind
> I have failed or forgotten to say
> year after year.

And by instinct the words come—a whirlwind of gathering force
carrying her further into that lonely place she has occupied in
our imaginations—half-prophetic, half-mad, but "attending" to
herself at the poem's crescendo:

> only car for the many-lived, unending
> forms in which she finds herself
> becoming now the shard of broken glass
> slicing light in a corner, dangerous
> to flesh, now the plentiful, soft leaf
> that wrapped round the throbbing finger, soothes the wound;
> and now the stone foundation rockshelf further
> forming underneath everything that grows.

The Dream of a Common Language is the work, as it says on the
book jacket, of a "necessary" writer, one to whom it is often
painful and guilt provoking to listen. But she is much more than
a conscience, much more than a rhetorician. She is, with this

book, the embodiment of a kind of alternative poetics, a new time asesthetic that changes our language—how we listen and speak to ourselves. We can hear a future in her words. Unlike almost every other contemporary poet, she does not fear looking ahead—so far ahead sometimes she seems like an anachronism. He loneliness and her strength both derive from a similar place. She is frightened and brave, an "explorer." She is not a female Whitman, though her themes occasionally echo his. She keeps on and nearly succeeds at loving herself. She commits sins of excess. Her great love is unrequited; she believes that this will change. I believe her. The name of her new language is *woman,* and, if we're smart, we'll listen to it, even learn to speak it.

Lingua Materna: The Speech of Female History

Sylvia Plath, on meeting Adrienne Rich (whose work she greatly admired) in spring 1958, drew her new acquaintance in her journal this way: "Adrienne Cecile Rich . . . all vibrant short black hair, great sparkling black eyes and a tulip-red umbrella: honest, frank, forthright and even opinionated." That last adjective packs a little irony in 1985 for anyone remotely familiar with the poetry and politics of Adrienne Rich.

With *The Fact of a Doorframe* we confront thirty-four years of the "opinionated" poems of this complex and controversial writer, who began as poet-ingenue, polite copyist of Yeats and Auden, wife and mother. She has progressed in life (and in her poems, which remain intimately tied to her life's truth) from young widow and disenchanted formalist to spiritual and rhetorical convalescent to feminist leader, lesbian separatist, and doyenne of a newly defined female literature—becoming finally a Great Outlaw Mother. Her progress makes that Cambridge afternoon so long ago, with the two ambitious young poets politely sizing each other up, portentous as an old newsreel. Both addressed what is referred to as "a woman's lot," both became legends, but the one with the opinions has survived to her fifty-sixth year.

The next question, of course, looking at thirty-four years of

From a review of *The Fact of a Doorframe: Poems Selected and New 1950–1984* by Adrienne Rich, in *New York Times Book Review,* January 20, 1985, Copyright © 1985 by The New York Times Co. Reprinted by Permission.

her work is: have Adrienne Rich's poems survived her opinions? At times her partisan views have outdistanced her poetry's inventiveness, but we must also consider that she has redefined *partisan,* for what other poet in recent memory has spoken of creating a new language, unearthing a lost history, rewriting the sacred texts for her cause? If her tasks sound grandiose, her stated intent does not; it's almost funny. "To do something very common, in my own way."

The Fact of a Doorframe has an imposed, retrospective order, as if to give cohesion to autobiography, a common ground to the poems. But her placement of the title poem gives us more insight into her sense of personal history than do her introduction, her notes or the selection and arrangement of the work. Dated 1974, the poem is placed on the frontispiece, a door in a doorframe, inviting us into the nine books (two new since her last volume of selected poems appeared ten years ago) and a quantity of older and recent uncollected poems. The title poem is about the suffering of entering—birth, death, writing—and it refers to the head of the talking mare, Falada, from the fairy tale "The Goose Girl." The mare's head was a kind of poetical conscience for the goose girl (in reality a princess), expressing the heart's guilt, putting into language another's suffering.

> and in a human voice
> *If she could see thee now, thy mother's heart would break*
> *said the head*
> of Falada

Like the head of the magical talking mare, poetry has always been both dilemma and animating principle for Adrienne Rich: "Now, again, poetry / violent, arcane, common." Her writing has always lifted her naturally toward a unifying transcendental vision, a dream, but a dream simultaneously wrenched and weighted by its moral embodiment, called by her at different stages: love, truth, integrity, commonality, silence. She is a true metaphysical poet, made didactic by force of her politics. She cannot proceed without her principles (and who would ask it of her?), but the dialectical struggle that ensues between her heart and her imagination places her among the suffering she describes. The world she aspires to naturally in her poetry is not the world she must embrace for now. She writes in "North American Time": "But underneath the grandiose idea / is the thought that what I must engage . . . / is meant to break my heart and reduce me to silence."

She has been, from the beginning, a poet of pathos. Even the highly formal and imitative volumes "A Change of World" (1951) and "The Diamond Cutters" (1955) endlessly tied and retied their charming lyricism to notions of truth. But in "Moving in Winter," an uncollected poem from 1957, we begin to see a bolder integration of pathos. Where love has grown disillusioned, and truth simultaneously more commanding, this young poet of formal melody admits an insistent counterpoint (that of a wronged sensibility), and the poem is "shocked" into being:

> Their life, collapsed like unplayed cards,
> is carried piecemeal through the snow:
> Headboard and footboard now, the bed
> where she has lain desiring him
> where overhead his sleep will build
> its canopy to smother her once more.

The poem *is* its trauma. The regular gait of the four-stress line is rattled by her use of the offbeat, oppositional rhythm of *headboard and footboard now* and *canopy*. The separated bed is borne over the snow in a funeral march for intimacy; the poem mocks its own formality and the marriage, like its bed, splits apart before our eyes. What fuels the poem (besides the skillful argument between form and content) is the poignant tug of war between anger and tenderness. It is this kind of poem, the dance of opposites, that she does best.

There are many places in Adrienne Rich's work in which anger has won the tug of war, and not to her advantage. Nonetheless, this furious passage from the poem "Snapshots of a Daughter-in-law" works well: "The argument *ad feminam,* all the old knives / that have rusted in my back, I drive in yours, / *ma semblable, my soeur!*"The outraged observation approaches glee in the punch line borrowed from Baudelaire and is more effective at its offhand feminization of "male" language than the following "revision" of Portia's speech, from "Natural Resources": "But gentleness is active / gentleness swabs the crusted stump." The poem loses it dramatic tension as it degenerates into name-calling, with gentleness "bearing witness calmly / against the predator, the parasite."

Conversely, a rare moment of equanamity is denied in a more recent poem, "The Spirit of Place," in which "the undamaged planet seems to turn / like a bowl of crystal," in Elizabethan beauty and order. The communion of the poet with nature is undercut by a political vigilance that distrusts even the stars: "All the figures up there look violent to me / as a pogrom on Christmas Eve in some old country." In passages like these, she loses her own argument and the language goes flat, victimized by her ideological impatience.

But at other times her dialectical fire produces poems of transcendent beauty. Her music has not forsaken her, after all these years, through all the transformations. It is at its most versatile, moving from an antiphonal, biblical time in "Upcountry"— "unable to take forgiveness neither do you / give mercy"—to the resonant bittersweetness of old rhymes in "The Spirit of Place":

> Over the hills in Shutesbury, Leverett
> driving with you in spring   road
> like a streambed unwinding downhill
> fiddlehead ferns uncurling
> spring peepers ringing sweet and cold.

Inhabiting the spirit of the "savage child" of Aveyron, she desires to "go back so far there is another language," but earlier, identifying with Emily Dickinson, she wished to "have it out . . . on [her] own premises." That contradiction has never been clearly resolved in her work, though the confusion has been relegated to the theoretical. On that level, and with a Derridean censure of the nostalgic, she has "gone back" to the premises of a new, female language. This language, much heralded in the collections *Diving into the Wreck* (1973) and *The Dream of a Common Language* (1978), and set against the old "written-out" tongue with its dialect of sexually biased metaphor, turns out to be the lost voices of female history.

In several recent poems she appears as a kind of medium, passing along to us the diurnal thoughts of deceased women. In these long, jagged-edged, epistolary, "uncreated" passages, she manages to talk and listen at once (a uniquely maternal gift) to Emily Dickinson, the novelist Ellen Glasgow, her grandmothers, Ethel Rosenberg, Susan B. Anthony, and Mary Jane Colter (a turn-of-the-century architect). These pieces are very even. The sections to Dickinson are outspoken, empathetic, and apt. The poem to Ethel Rosenberg is awkward and unconvincing in its sentiment.

What I like about them is their wintry but undefeated feel, like letters written home by a longtime expatriate. Adrienne rich is speaking her *lingua materna;* she has answered her timeless question, "With whom do you believe your lot is cast?"; the last thirty-four years have been filled with change. Still, she is restless. She writes in "North American Time":

> When my dreams showed signs
> of becoming
> politically correct . . .
> then I began to wonder.

The wonder saves her. For a poet whose acts of survival have sometimes become "rituals of self-hatred," as she says of all women, this wonder is the source of poetry.

We are going to hear even more from this remarkable poet, whose passionate excesses, whose brilliant, terrifying leaps of faith often affect us more deeply than the ingrown successes of our assemblage of "approved" poets. The last poem in *The Fact of a Doorframe* ends with the line "and I start to speak again," and we have no doubt that she will. Sylvia Plath noticed it a long time ago. This is a poet with opinions.

The Romantic Heresy

The late-twentieth-century poetic imagination is in crisis, Eavan Boland says in *Object Lessons,* her new collection of essays. The word *crisis* is, alas, sorely familiar to the reader of contemporary American poetry. Indeed, the terrain of poetry has been commandeered as one of the battlegrounds upon which literary skirmishes representing larger culture wars are routinely fought. We have weathered a storm of aesthetic/political blitzkrieg: *McPoem, neo-formalism vs. free verse, The Death of Poetry, lyric vs. narrative, feminism vs. phallocentrism, The Canon vs. Multiculturalism, the Balkanization of Poetry vs. Eurocentrism, the critic vs. the author, Poetry Slam vs. The Academy, and Harold Bloom vs. Everybody.*

Boland's interest in these struggles is keen but cool. Her own argument constructs itself outside this arena of conflict or perhaps more deeply within it than previously imaginable—indeed, it might be said that she writes from the point of view of the battlefield itself. The crisis of the imagination is present within the poem, she says, and the "drama of expression" that shapes the self of the poet.

This is what her book seems to be "about," though its style and structure are also its subject: an object lesson. But demonstrating what? There is not much new in the insight that poetry and its "grammar" are influenced by cultural forces that both prefigure and lend context to literary language. This ground has been trod flat by ideological linguists, structuralists from Saussure to Chomsky to Barthes to feminist revisionists, all tak-

From a review of Eavan Boland's *Object Lessons: The Life of the Woman and the Poet in Our Time* in *The Nation* Company, LP, Copyright © April 24, 1995.

ing sides as to how linguistic usage—discourse—in literary forms incarnates the cultural process. What *is* new here is that the heavily trafficked ground is being mined by a poet, casting her poet's eye before us like a miner's light, intent on "digging us out" from under the weight of pious assumptions about the imagination that end up subverting its history. She is exposing a rift in the imagination, a great glittering crack in our power to make images, that's been around since before "The Twa Corbies." Imagination has not been the great healing force that Coleridge and the Romantics proposed but an energy flawed by human evasion and limitation. Here Boland is a kind of creative empiricist, operating in the spirit of Eluard, whose statement "there is another world, but it is in this one" she quotes. Boland, shining her light on the cave walls, urges to "enter the interior of the poem and reinscribe certain powerful and customary relations between object and subject."

What sounds like a form of chilly revisionism is not: this is a poet devoted to Yeats, respectful of the past. Her demand is not that we dismiss or diminish this past but that the argument be relocated within the lyric moment, deep in the fissure, to resee the poem's "strategy of possession" as "an act of rescue." Unlike Adrienne Rich, who dived into the wreck of human relations to view the ruin of the past and reject it, Boland does not wish to move from "one simplification to another" but to demonstrate the "field of force" in which women are caught.

For it is of women she writes—in particular, the separation between the ideas of "woman" and "poet" and the dual consciousness that this split gives to women. In a momentous literary turnaround in our own time women are given a unique opportunity to restate the givens of the poem: once most commonly cast as an object within the poem, they are now its authors. Boland writes:

> If I had to name this inscription, I would say that the sexual and erotic were joined in a powerful sign which marked the very center of poetry. I knew without yet being able to reason it out that this was one of the oldest, most commanding fixities in poetry, responsible for the beauty of the erotic object in the poem. But also for its silence and agelessness.

The evidence Boland offers for this view is her own life and the country of her imagination, a kind or terra incognita that is (interchangeably) her native Ireland, a childhood spent in exile, the ordinary life of a woman and her separate life as a poet.

In a prose style so lyrical, spare, and elegiac that it rivals poetry, she draws us into personal memory, autobiographical anecdote, and family history, which, rather than confirming her identity, interrogate it at every turn, witnessing her uncertain choices in the process of creating a writerly self.

By weaving autobiography into analysis, Boland cleverly embodies her argument, spinning an object lesson made of her self and her "story." The broken iconography of a "lost" grandmother's life, an unidentified overgrown grave, a signature on a death certificate, a collective memory of an eviction, shadow her own childhood exile from a sensuous, dreamily evocative Dublin to the formal, foreign, inhospitable milieu of 1950s London, where her father was sent as ambassador from Ireland.

Boland chronicles an early lesson on how power in language (and attendant silence) is enforced through the authority of syntax:

> A teacher was marshaling children here and there, dividing those who were taking buses from those who were being collected. "I amn't taking the bus," I said. I was six or seven then, still within earshot of another way of speaking. But the English do not use that particular construction. It is an older usage. If they contract the verb and the negative, they say, "I'm not." Without knowing, I had used that thing for which the English reserve a visceral dislike: their language, loaded and aimed by the old enemy. The teacher whirled around, corrected my grammar; her face set, her tone cold. "You're not in Ireland now" was what she said.

What Boland further implies, but does not remark, is that the English usage favors emphasis on the nominative subjective, the kingly "I," flattening out the "to be" verb. She is correct not to point this out—her subject is not the power and privilege of British syntax (though it would be hard to find a better example of a "strategy of possession" versus "an act of rescue")—for she is steadfastly talking about her life as it applies to the making of poetry. And in this context she moves us gracefully from London back to Ireland, where she considers Irish nationalism and the poet's lot.

Her return to Ireland as a young woman (to attend Trinity College) figured powerfully in her fancy as a return to all that was early lost. In fact, she discovered that true homecoming was an impossibility; she could find no entry into the past. She hadn't the set of references, the "Irish" experience. English educated, well traveled, a fairly serious Latin scholar, and, finally a fledgling poet, she found herself exchanging one set of "constructs" for another. She began to sense that there is something that is kept inexpressible, something deemed "outside" poetic experience.

Ireland, Boland says, gives us a "vivid" example of poetic nationalism and how it evolves not from real life but from culture and not from the "harsh awakenings" but from the "old dreams":

> The real issue went deeper. When I read these simplifications of women, I felt there was an underlying fault in Irish poetry, almost a geological weakness. All good poetry depends on an ethical relation between imagination and image. Images are not ornaments; they are truths. When I read about Cathleen in Houlihan or the Old Woman of the Roads or Dark Rosaleen, I felt a necessary ethical relation was in danger of being violated over and over again, that a merely ornamental relation between imagination and image was being handed on from poet to poet, from generation to generation.

Every so often, like a composer underscoring a leitmotif, Boland interrupts herself and conducts the reader back to a lit room. In this room we see a woman alone—Boland herself at different ages, thinking or writing. Sometimes she is a child learning Latin and dreaming; at another glimpse she is a young writer sitting before the empty lamp-lit page, her pen and coffee mug on the desk before her; yet another turn reveals a young mother listening to the breathing of her sleeping children before taking up her pen. She seems to want to etch this image for all time on the reader's consciousness, till it becomes a new emblem. She lifts it up to the light, interrogates it, but does not desire that this image become romanticized.

> The Romantic Heresy, as I have chosen to call it, is not romanticism proper, although it is related to it "Before Wordsworth," writes Lionel Trilling, "poetry had a subject. After Wordsworth, its prevalent subject was the poet's own subjectivity."

This shift in poetry, she says, was responsible for much that was fresh and revitalizing in nineteenth-century poetry. But it was also responsible for the descent into self-consciousness and self-invention.

Further, this type of "debased romanticism" is rooted in a "powerful subliminal" suggestion that poets are significant not because they write poems but because they have "poetic feelings" about "poetic experiences." This tautology implies that there is a hierarchy to human experience, and at the bottom of the order is "ordinary" life, a life separate from the poetic/erotic. So she comes to her conclusion, revealing the fault in the earth:

> I have also argued that far from making a continuum, the contemporary poem as written by women can actually separate the sexual and erotic, and separate, also, the sexual motif from that of poetic expression. And that when a woman poet does this, a circuit of power represented by their fusion is disrupted. The erotic object can be rescued and restored: from silence to expression, from the erotic to the sensory. When this happens, beautiful, disturbing tones are free to enter the poem. Poetry itself comes to the threshold of changes which need not exclude or diminish the past but are bound to reinterpret it.

Readers familiar with Boland's poetry know these "beautiful, disturbing tones" from her work. In *Outside History* (1990) a poem titled "The Journey" takes place in the margin of the sixth book of *The Aeneid*. The narrator-poet falls asleep over her book and is taken to the underworld by Sappho, where they encounter (just at the edge of the plot) the souls of infants who have died untimely deaths from cholera, typhus, croup, and diphtheria, who float, "suckling darkness." The poet asks Sappho to allow her to write about these souls, asks to be their "witness." Sappho replies, "What you have seen is beyond speech / beyond song, only not beyond love."

This response, beautiful and disturbing, disrupts the great opera of the sixth book as Sappho speaks again, offering "knowledge of silence" as a means of understanding. Boland's point here is not to rewrite an epic; she is attempting to shift the ground of what the poem takes for granted. The poet returns to her own study in her own house, where "the rain was grief in arrears; my children / slept the last dark out safely and I wept."

Boland is clearly a woman who does not fear controversy. Statements like the earlier argument about separating the sexual and the erotic, misread, will excite more debate—but those who attend closely will not miss the truth of what *Object Lessons* is saying. It is not like any other book in memory: inspired, relentless, deliberately and eloquently hand-drawn.

"I am neither a separatist nor a postfeminist," she says. And, more poignantly: "I want a poem I can grow old in. I want a poem I can die in." This cry echoes the unforgettable lyric cries of the alienated spirit throughout poetry—Hopkins's "O thou lord of life, send my roots rain," Herbert's "O that I once past changing were," and Dickinson's "My Life had stood—a Loaded Gun—."

I want a poem I can grow old in. I want a poem I can die in. Until women can step free of the charmed poetic atmosphere, the precedent that "stops time," they cannot grow old; they cannot die inside the poem. They remain ageless, beautiful, with the "power to kill, without the power to die."

Eavan Boland is dead serious. The battlefield has spoken; the Muse is packing her bag; the woman in the room turns to speak to us:

> I stood at the center of the lyric moment itself, in a mesh of colors, sensualities and emotions that were equidistant from poetic convention and political feeling alike. Technically and aesthetically I became convinced that if I could only detach the lyric mode from traditional romantic elitism and the new feminist angers, then I would be able at last to express that moment.

In that "equidistance" the lighted room floats up like a new moon. In it we see a woman writing.

Revising the Future

Tradition is a matter of much wider significance. It cannot be inherited, and if you want it you must obtain it by great labour. It involves, in the first place, the historical sense, which we may call nearly indispensable to anyone who would continue to be a poet beyond his twenty-fifth year; and the historical sense involves a perception not only of the pastness of the past but of its presence; the historical sense compels a man to write not merely with his own generation in his bones, but with a feeling that the whole of the literature of Europe from Homer and within it the whole of literature of his country has a simultaneous existence and composes a simultaneous order. This historical sense, which is a sense of the timeless as well as of the temporal together is what makes a writer traditional. And it is at the same time what makes a writer acutely conscious of his place in time, of his own contemporaneity.[1]

I used to read this passage as if it were some sort of papal bull—T. S. Eliot ex cathedra—allowing the uninitiated a glimpse of the Covenant. Only lately has it occurred to me that what he's describing is something quite familiar. Familiar, that is, to poets who, after all, truck in awe. He's delineating the poetic process: which requires that we step out of time, confront an essentially mysterious universe, then recreate it in language. But why does this process, mystical as it may be, have to carry the weight of generations of literary precursors? That's a lot of people to crowd into one inspiration: a little like those mindless fraternity gags, twenty people in a telephone booth. And all that "historical sense," "generation in the bones" stuff: I doubt that Eliot himself really believed that. We can say with certainty, reading

From *Where We Stand; Women Poets on Literary Tradition*, ed. by Sharon Bryan (New York: W. W. Norton, 1993).

his poems, that he felt the power and timelessness of the poem, but the voice here is not that of Eliot the poet. This voice rather shamelessly dissembles: the rhetoric sounds judicious but is emotional. This voice idealizes the initiate's "passage" into what seems to be a glamorous fiction of the New Criticism, an appeal for the depersonalization of art (which he likens later in the essay and rather too enthusiastically—in true modernist style— to "the conditions of science") and his model for the simultaneous sublimation and aggrandizement of the poet's ego.

The first time I read "Tradition and the Individual Talent," as a young poet, I did not feel left out by Eliot's clear summons to the *man* who is poet, because I believed (and I *still* believe) (à la Virginia Woolf) that the imagination was androgynous. Therefore, I assumed, Eliot *must* have meant to include all of us, male and female poets alike, in that one "man." And, though I'd never experienced any such thing, maybe there *were* poets who felt Homer's breath on their necks as they lifted a pen?

Now I read these words, and other, darker tones surface beneath the modulated official voice: for example, Eliot detaches himself from his own *drama* (this is, after all, a literary séance, a real table rapper, dredging up the Old Guys); he offers us an oddly mechanical reduction of an ecstatic process and then gets really clinical: he dequantifies Time, as in the popularized versions of Einstein's relativity theory. Linear time becomes spatial time, or "timelessness" in time, as he puts it.

This historical sense (time *and* timelessness) provides Eliot's contemporary poet simultaneously with equality to and primacy over the past. The past is made manifest in the present; thus, the historical is generative. Eliot says that tradition cannot be inherited, but the "labour" (!) that he insists is necessary to obtain it seems *given* and magical, like Arthur's freeing of Excalibur from the stone. The magic here involves conjuring the poet's "family tree" in a second: the literary equivalent of the selection process in genetics. What's avoided here is finally most present: the buried motif of birth, the birth of the poem. For what other metaphor, though hopelessly clichéd, still best represents the creative process, from inspiration (conception) through "delivery"? That Eliot stops short of it, that he will not name it, only serves to enhance its presence. One is tempted to conclude that in the absence of the Other (code word for women), men are forced to give birth themselves—to creation myths like this.

Harold Bloom offers advice here. He does not think that "sexual distaste or anxiety was at the root of Eliot's aversion to his own experience of poetic origins. Rather, he *dissimulated as all good poets seem to need to mystify in this area*" (my emphasis).

Well, yes. All good poets seem to need to mystify, those slippery tricksters. But this need seems to me to have less to do with protective camouflage and more to do with the poem's relationship to time. Eliot's concern with the past is familiar: he wants to set up a sanctioned order of succession. He is less concerned with the poem's natural affinity to a more inclusive *future*. But if it is possible to believe that every poem is a beginning, a moment of origin, then merely signaling the past into the present seems an incomplete gesture. As the poet H. D. said, in describing Freud's genius: he could make the "dead" live, but he could also *make the future live in the present*—thus releasing the pain of the analysand attached to either.

The future *in* poetry, or within an individual poem, is not necessarily connected to Poetry's own future. Every poet sitting down to write confronts the "blank space," paces on the cliff's edge. The future for us is inspiration, imagination—the silence before and after the narrative: what we move toward. Wordsworth spoke of the poet's need to look before and after him, and Shelley's poet-"seer" instructed politicians; Keats described negative capability, the poet's ability to exist in uncertainty. Are we, now, still influenced by modernism's iconoclastic sense of the past? The modernist infatuation with classicism proved to be little more than an excuse for Hellenizing the fish-and-chips peddler and the so-called reclaiming of the common, the utilitarian, even the scientific, simply broke the future into fragments of contradiction. Despite the Futurists, the Vorticists, and Pound's cry to "make it new," there was no connection with what was to follow. In fact, there are those who would argue that modernism destroyed the postmodern future in which we now live. Eliot said: "the poet should know everything that has been accomplished in poetry . . . since its beginnings . . . in order to know what he is doing himself. He should be aware of all the metamorphoses of poetry that illustrate the stratifications of history that cover savagery."[2] And Eliot, when asked by Stephen Spender to describe the future, also foresaw this savagery *before* him: "internecine fighting . . . people killing each other in the streets." From my present perspective in the city of Los Angeles I find him most clairvoyant. But this bestial Tomorrow, as apprehended by Eliot, was not so different, for him, from what had come before. He was a man frightened of both father and son.

The female body has been appropriated for every kind of trope lately, and I desperately wish to avoid imposing yet another gender theory on it. Yet it's in our minds: woman, birth, and future, that the Other, the feminine, might provide a healing alternative here—and to resist this trope might seem to deny the source of our imagining. But resist it we must. It is just this kind of "temporary aesthetic manoeuvre," as Eavan Boland points out, that avoids the truth.[3] In fact, Eliot himself, in *Criterion*, referred to the poem as a "dark embryo." Extending the prenatal conceit, he said he was most concerned with making the past live in the *present* in a "reintegrated" manner. And, finally, when all is said and done, he is less concerned with the integration of the past; he says it is the present that affords the most possibility of literary bonding: "writers who are not merely connected by a tradition in time, but who are related so as to be in the light of *eternity contemporaneous*."[4]

"Eternity contemporaneous" sounds like a Catholic prep school, and in a way it was. Eliot acquired this take on the present at Oxford, when he wrote a thesis on the "associationist" philosopher F. H. Bradley. Far more than from Imagism or Pound, Eliot derived his poetics from Bradley, including his notion of the objective correlative. One of Bradley's tenets was that Feeling everywhere is trying to "reintegrate" itself into larger and more complete "wholes." (Everybody's conscious mind confronted these floating fragments of Feeling, but it took a poet's sensibility to fuse them.) The poem, for Eliot, linked the savage and the civilized; what psychoanalysis tried to do for the individual consciousness, literature could accomplish for the collective mind.

Eliot's obsession with the eternal contemporaneous begs the question about facing what is to come. (It is indeed a temporary aesthetic maneuver.) The past is always depicted as *arriving*, ongoing—there is no tomorrow. With the past running in tandem with the present, we are doomed to repeat a history of fathers and sons ad infinitum; we are doomed to the stratifications of savagery and civilization, the endlessly mirrored self. Again, the temptation is to say that only by *getting past* the past—in effect, giving birth to another—can we redefine our relationship to poetry. I was tempted, in an earlier essay, to make such a claim.

In 1979 I reviewed Adrienne Rich's *The Dream of a Common Language* for *Parnassus* magazine, in a piece called "Backward into the Future." In my review I discussed Rich's countermanding of the "historical order" in poetry, which was "the habit of viewing each poem written in the language as 'heir presumptive' to the tradition." It struck me that the "matrilinear heritage" does not seem to proceed "hierarchically" but "horizontally," as underscored by Rich's image of women passing a seed hand to hand. I quoted Woolf: "Yet I am now and then haunted by some semi-mystic very profound life of a woman, which shall be told on one occasion; and time shall be utterly obliterated; future shall somehow blossom out of the past."

I felt that Woolf was speaking to all women as well as to her "spark" of *Mrs. Dalloway*; I felt I was on to something:

> Regarding "tradition," perhaps the aversion of many American poets to what is called "political poetry" may be, in part, fear of an altered sense of time's passage, fear, in particular, of a future. Certainly the desire to locate and define the past that obsesses contemporary poetry does seem predominantly male. The themes of the search for the lost father, the death of the father (heralded in the oedipal criticism of Harold Bloom), the son's rite of passage, and nostalgia for the nuclear family are all cloaked in ready-to-wear pathos.
>
> That is why Rich has asked us to "honor the risk" of her dream exploration out of time—accompanying that expedition requires us to move out of male history and tradition.[5]

The rather bald claims of this earlier essay, if reductionist, are sincere. The notion of time, and women writers freeing themselves from its contraints, seems as central to me now as it did then. It is important to know the past and the women writers of the past but not with the sense of "civilizing savagery" that Eliot's tradition imposes. It is important to know these poets in the context of a *future* entirely outside history and its expectations. All poets believe in the timelessness of their art; it is women who are required to face this flow without a literary trust fund. It is precisely because of noninheritance—because we seem to be bastards, paupers, black sheep—that we are, at the millenium (or at whatever moment; look at Dickinson!), so free to face possibilities.

In 1979 I was interested in confronting the difference, if there is one, between Eliot's Past, or Eternal Contemporaneous, and a different kind of future. Now I'm not. Now it seems to me that "living within" a great poem by a woman might provide the best "future." Eavan Boland has written a poem (from her book *Outside History*) called "The Journey."[6] The poem begins with a woman's voice, a mother's voice—"chastising" the past in the poem. "There has never been," she says " a poem to an antibiotic"; and "somewhere a poet is wasting / his sweet uncluttered meters on the obvious / emblem instead of the real thing." Every day, she says, "language gets less / for the task and we are less with the language."

The speaker then falls asleep over her books, and Sappho steps off the page the poet's been drowsing over. The dreaming poet is led by Sappho into the twilight world (where Virgil has led Dante in the *Aeneid*) where the souls of infants who have died untimely deaths from "cholera, typhus, croup, diphtheria" float "suckling darkness." The poet pleads with Sappho to allow her to write about these souls, asking to be their "witness." Sappho replies, "what you have seen is beyond speech / beyond song, only not beyond love."

Thus Boland collapses time, guided by a great poet, into and out of the temporal, following Eliot's dictum, but the poetry (the poem itself) that derives from this journey teaches a lesson we have never learned in history—or the history of poetry. "Remember it, you will remember it," says Sappho. Then she seems to acknowledge a kind of "tradition": "There are not many of us; you are dear / and stand beside me as my own daughter." But it is Sappho's final revelation that provides new instruction, sets aside the ideal of literary transmission as ego: "I have brought you here so you will know forever—the silences in which are our beginnings,—in which we have an origin like water."

Silence? To learn silence? To understand that the experience of suffering may be beyond speech or song? But only learnable through love? That language may be "less" than the task of loving? (Elizabeth Bishop to Robert Lowell, on the occasion of his appropriating his wife's letters for his own poems: "Art just isn't worth that much.")

And Boland's stance here defies its own dictum about silence but with profoundly different effect than, say, the "still point of the turning world." The poet does indeed bear witness to the infant souls, as well as Sappho's commentary. We do stay "in speech," "in song," "in language," the poem remains very much a poem (written in traditional formal style), but the solar system has shifted within the poem, and we have a different "sun"; we are asked to *learn* silence, to listen to it, *prior* to language—not beyond love.

It is a temptation: the desire to start over clean, as women and writers—a whole new aesthetic. But it doesn't work that way. We do live in history; we have, all of us, served our apprenticeships—studying male poets, male literary history. There is much beauty and pain and truth in what we've learned, and there are damaging lies. The future we reinvent is dependent on our reinterpretation of what's preceded us. Boland's poem, though it begins in accusation and sorrow, ends up powerfully refiguring a vision of the *Aeneid,* ends up rewriting the lessons drawn from the epic past.

What I've written here are musings: outside of theory. That is to say, they offer not a strategy of women's poetry, nor a new tradition, but my own "history" of the future that is still happening to us: the poem itself.

NOTES

1. T. S. Eliot, "Tradition and the Individual Talent", 38.
2. *Atheneum* (Oct. 17, 1919), p. 1036
3. *American Poetry Review* (March/April 1990), pp. 32–38.

4. Stephen Spender, *The Thirties and After* (New York: Vintage, 1967), p. 202.

5. "Backwards into the Future," *Parnassus: Poetry in Review* (Spring/ Summer 1979), p. 81.

6. Eavan Boland, *Outside History* (New York: W. W. Norton & Co., 1990), pp. 93–96.

Laura Riding Roughshod

William Carlos Williams called her a "prize bitch," while Virginia Woolf dismissed her as a "damned bad poet." Louise Bogan thought she should be "slammed in the eye"; Dorothy L. Sayers declared her writing "abracadabra—a hypnotic rumble of stupefying polysyllables." Dudley Fitts reared far back, pronouncing her with "few equals" when it can to "browbeating an audience into conviction by sheer force of arrogance, among any poets living or dead." Judging by the caliber of her enemies, we might assume that Laura Riding did *something* right.

Deborah Baker's new biography of Riding, the aptly titled "*In Extremis,*" in no way denies the right Riding did. (Her biography arrives in the midst of Riding's resurrection: the reissuing of four of her books, setting her in a bright revisionist spotlight as another forgotten female genius pulled from the rubble of modernism.)

Laura Riding grew up, undaunted, in impoverished circumstances: she was an immigrant tailor's daughter, born in 1901 in New York City. She imbibed much of her father's impassioned socialism—enough for a lifelong argument with the status quo. She won a scholarship to Cornell, began to write poetry, won a poetry prize offered by the Fugitives (the group of Southern

Review of *In Extremis: The Life of Laura Riding* by Deborah Baker; and four books by Laura (Riding) Jackson: *First Awakenings: The Early Poems of Laura Riding* edited by Elizabeth Friedmann, Alan J. Clark, and Robert Nye; *Laura Riding: Selected Poems of Laura Riding; The Word "Woman" and Other Related Writings* edited by Elizabeth Friedmann and Alan J. Clark; and *Four Unposted Letters to Catherine* from *The New York Times Book Review,* November 28, 1993.

gentleman poets that included Allen Tate and Robert Penn Warren), and ended up exerting real (if unacknowledged) influence on their traditionalist aesthetic. She sailed in 1925 in the modernist exodus to Europe (at the invitation of Robert Graves, who'd discovered, reading a poem of hers, that they were destined to be together), and in her next fourteen expatriate years she wrote an astonishing number of books: poetry, fiction, and philosophical essays.

She also collaborated with Graves, most notably on *A Survey of Modernist Poetry,* published in 1927, which some critics believe launched the New Criticism, and on the tiny Seizen Press, which made them publishers of some influence. Her early philosophical musings turned into a feverish epistemological hunt for Truth: among other manifestoes she issued a universal call to arms for women, exhorting them to reassert their power as a "source," "more real than God, more real than man." As self-styled visionary, she became a crusader for language protocols intended to abolish war through exact speech. She fought the sexism of editors and publisher, and of her own male friends and lovers, who were not above usurping her ideas (Riding claimed Graves's *White Goddess* borrowed heavily from her own thinking). Their time together was volatile, and remains the subject of controversy; nevertheless she and Graves prospered intellectually, drawing many admiring young poets and writers to their home in the tiny village of Deyá, on the island of Majorca. In 1991, the last year of her life, Laura Riding, now ninety, was awarded the prestigious Bollingen Prize for her "lifelong contribution" to poetry.

The disparity between the snide comments of contemporaries and an ideal literary life is, of course, the biographer's native realm. For Deborah Baker, however, this stretch of Riding territory is mined ground, fraught with obstacles to understanding what biographers call the real life of their subjects. Riding herself appears the most persistent obstacle—not only because of contradictory and highly disturbing accounts of her character and personal life provided by herself and others, but because she cultivated a perversely protean literary identity that defined everything she did. The events of writers' biographies often take a back seat to the driving life of their imaginations. In Riding's case imagination stood on the gas pedal and floored it.

First Awakenings: The Early Poems of Laura Riding, a cache of some two-hundred poems left behind when she sailed abroad, reveals the pre-expatriate Laura, "Dimensions," among other poems, shows that although young she was already fierce in confident self-appraisal:

> Measure me by myself
> And not by time or love or space
> Or beauty. Give me this last grace:
> That I may be on my low stone
> A gage unto myself alone.
> I would not have these old faiths fall
> To prove that I was nothing at all.

In other early poems Riding fiddles impatiently with prosodic form: the forced obvious rhymes and metronomic stresses barely contain this tiger in a cage of Georgian politesse. When she bends the bars, as she does in a poem, "Addresses," we hear the straight-talk cadences of the modern age and beyond; she prefigures Sexton, Plath, even Berryman:

> Father, I have begun to think.
> Come and listen at my head.
> It is frightful, like being dead
> and having to hide
> Everything in you that was once outside.

There were several "Lauras," as Ms. Baker illustrates in her biography—some lived, some died. The precocious Laura, Ms. Baker suggests, dissolved into one of Riding's "successive identities" in a "roundabout story" of the "perplexing creatures who sprang repeatedly from this woman's head." Riding's mob of aliases reflected not just her marriages but also this spontaneous regeneration. In the course of her life she went from Laura Reichenthal (her maiden name) to Laura Gottschalk to Laura Riding Gottschalk to Laura Riding to Laura (Riding) Jackson. Hart Crane dubbed her "Laura Riding Roughshod."

Riding had an unfortunate lifelong compulsion to explain herself. She published long explications of her psycholiterary

development—progressive revelations that led to an official re-
nunciation of poetry in 1941, when she declared that poetry
blocked "truth's ultimate verbal harmonies." Perhaps the deeper,
sadder truth was that she had sacrificed her talent to her moral
crusade. Her poems, filled with abstract posturings, turned to
linguistic curios. In *Laura Riding: Selected Poems in Five Sets,* pub-
lished in Britain in 1970 with a preface by the author, and just
reissued, the poems' arrangement mirrors the achronological
thematic approach of Mr. Baker's biography. The setting is irrele-
vant; what comes through, as here, from "That Ancient Line," is
the willed diminishment of a poet's voice.

> Indeed, between Act and Matter-of-Fact
> Was such consanguineous sympathy
> That the displeasure of the matronymic
> In the third generation of pure logic
> Did not detract from the authority
> Of this and later versions
> Of the original progenitive argument.

This hothouse style, impenetrable in places, also began to
characterize Riding's prose, which reads pretty much like a mi-
graine. Not much can excuse this style, but its excesses can be
understood. Times were tough for women artists. The gatekeep-
ers of culture, Pound and Eliot et al., weren't giving passes to
their female peers. Like many of her modernist sisters, Riding
was forced to employ desperate measures to insure the survival
of her reputation. Against what she perceived as Graves's aggres-
sive "pseudo-Hellenic" piracy (she called him a "literary robber
baron") she engendered her own obsessive mythos and hyper-
bolized her tone but lost her lyric gift.

Riding, naturally, had the right to use her talent however she
wished; what she never had was the right to rewrite history. Ms.
Baker is supremely sensitive to this fact; still it cannot go unno-
ticed that she is publishing this biography in a powerful climate
of resurgence and restoration. If Riding's age was resistant or
largely indifferent to women's writing, our own fin-de-siècle pre-
occupation is with righting shocking biases of the past: recover-
ing and mainstreaming marginalized writers. This gesture is as
inherently just as it is dangerous—an obvious concern being the

confusion of historical significance with literary substance. Riding's resurrection, in particular, raises many questions: whom do we canonize and why? And it raises *the* unasked question: are we operating in the absence of a criticism sufficiently detached to guard against her false inflation of reputation? This profusion of books by and about Riding backs a rather incautious principle: if self-testimony is art, then Riding is the most important writer of the twentieth century.

Ms. Baker notes in her introduction that "to judge Riding's life in those terms [by] which her male contemporaries sought to understand it . . . is inevitably to diminish and even condemn Laura Riding to myth, megalomania or marginality." On the other hand, she states that to judge Riding by the terms which she herself later renounced Graves and others is to "denounce and silence her." What to do?

Riding, Ms. Baker reiterates, "wanted her story told, but she wanted it to be hers. She admitted of no other or the possibility of others without malicious motive. The present work . . . was no exception." Indeed, Riding was still alive when Ms. Baker began her book; the fact that the biographer dispensed with a linear approach and chose to track the minotaur through the heady labyrinth of the Lauras suggests the importance to Ms. Baker of placating her subject. The sympathetic and ambitious scope of this technique gives us, on the one hand, a close-up sense of the bizarre raids Riding made on her own unconscious. Ms. Baker is particularly acute at decoding the eerie logic of these transformations.

On the other hand, her documentation of identity bending makes for odd transitions, missing dates and facts, long and lackluster digressions on peripheral characters, and timid critical inquiry. This is clearly not meant to be a scholarly biography, yet Ms. Baker's occasional judgments are intelligent, tonic and sorely needed in a life so devoid of critical context. She makes clear in her introduction that she never had any intention of "setting the record straight." But at the worst her self-effacement leads to an unconscious mimicking of Riding's own style at its most didactic and condescendingly animated—Mary Worth on acid:

With Maisie, Laura discussed literalism as it touched on educa-
tion; with Honor she explored a literal approach to novels. Julian
Symons was subjected to a "literal criticism" of his poems, which
involved severe questioning of his use of the word "hypotenuse."

This conflict between the impulse to collaborate and the
impulse to remain objective accounts for the muffledness of Ms.
Baker's style, the low volume of her conclusions.

The volume should have been turned up. Questions about
Riding far outdistance answers by the end of the book. Who,
after all, was this person? A madwoman or a literal-minded mys-
tic? And how do we assess her promising early poems, the odd
and sometimes splendid stories, the occasional brilliance of *The
Word* "WOMAN," and the pages and pages of mystification and
outrage that followed? How do we "re-call" this writer from the
margins and acknowledge her influence—as a major poet or a
provocative historical figure?

Did she really believe that she was God? Or, allowing for
modernist theatricality, God's actress—wrapped in her Mother-
Goosey outfits, carrying a parasol and, "no matter how hot it
was," sporting "jade-colored velvet gowns" and jeweled shoe
buckles, crowned with a gold wire tiara spelling LAURA?

Should Riding's vision of the future of women be questioned
(especially now that publishers are resurrecting her as a kind of
feminist oracle)? Even a cursory reading of her writings on this
topic makes it clear that her notion of women's influence em-
phasized the cultivation of depressingly familiar domestic vir-
tues. She could imagine a purely female cosmology, as she put
it, but deplored women in pants demanding their civil rights.

"Man is an outside, an outdoor creature—indoors is not a
serious idea to him," she wrote in "The Word 'Woman.' " "To
woman the whole universe is, ultimately, an indoor place; it is
her work to bring it all indoors. When woman becomes an
outdoor creature, either physically or intellectually, she is
'smart' . . . or clever or 'interesting,' but she ceases to be effec-
tive; she is no longer a comprehensive being."

And so, Riding wrote, "In fighting for full social liberation as if
it held the key for them to fullness of life and performance,
women are sealing themselves off from that of which they have, by

their woman-nature, pure, sure sensibility." *The Word "Woman": And Other Related Writings* contains the unpublished title essay (written in 1933–35 when she lived with Graves) as well as other essays and stories. Its appendix explodes with a gale force "personal commentary" on *The White Goddess* in her pass-the-machete style:

"It would not be enough to say of 'The White Goddess' that it is a . . . profession of poetic faith enacted with pseudo-naïve mind-immersing in glittering expanses of shallow poetic theorizing, into which is poured a foamy grandiose effusion of nothingish spiritualistics affecting learnedness in the meaning of *woman* in the cosmic totality; and to say that, as such, it is *deserved* by the modern intellectual populace that has emptied consciousness of a reality 'soul' and invited 'in,' for replacement, poetically inflated psychological theory and literarily and anthropologically recycled 'myth.'" . . . 'The White Goddess' is worse than this. It is a personal infliction, an act of revenge."

Despite all the attempts to rewrite her life, including her own, which emphasized her independence, Riding always relied openly on men and was extremely competitive with other women. When Graves invited her to Europe, she moved in with him and his wife, Nancy Nicholson. This ménage à trois (with the Graves children in the background) went on for some time (becoming a *ménage à quatre,* with the addition of Geoffrey Phibbs, an Irish poet and Riding's male muse), till Laura jumped out a window (her exit line: "Goodbye, chaps!") and broke her spine, nearly killing herself so that one of the Lauras could die and open the way to the future. As soon as Riding could walk again, she and Graves escaped to Majorca, leaving Nancy and the children behind.

Four Unposted Letters to Catherine, written to Graves's eight-year-old daughter, was published around this time (1930). The letters (ironically) were an airily composed primer on How to Live, how to avoid hypocrisies and pretensions.

On Majorca, avoiding hypocrisy, Riding came to the conclusion that sex was demeaning to women and stopped sleeping with Graves but found for him other women, whom she saw as an extension of the side of herself she had decided to withhold. When one of the women got pregnant, she was furious. She arranged an abortion and, according to the young woman, stood at the foot of the bed while the operation was performed.

When Riding returned to America in 1939, she and Graves moved in with the Schuyler Jackson family in New Hope, Pa. (Jackson was a journalist and early admirer of her work.) Laura promptly broke her celibacy vow with Jackson in his own home then launched a hair-raising character assassination campaign against his wife, Kit. She accused the woman of "witchcraft," using Inquisition documents to establish her guilt. Riding herself cultivated the image of a witch and regularly practiced "mind control"—how else explain her power over an entire family and their close friends, who, Ms. Baker tells us, ended up helping throw Kit Jackson's personal effects on a bonfire Riding had built after the poor woman had literally been driven to the insane asylum.

On the subject of Riding's short-loved friendship with Gertrude Stein, Ms. Baker says that "for both Riding and Stein . . . being women and being contemptuous of women had a special price." She notes that Stein's love for Alice Toklas helped contain her contempt for women and "kept the cost from being too great" but that Riding left herself no such "collateral." Riding ended up, in an unpublished essay, linking Stein's "perverse linguistic games" with her homosexuality, effectively denouncing her for her woman-love.

Such unsavory stuff is predictable fare in recent biographies. But in the cases of, say, Frost, Plath, Jean Stafford, and, most recently, Philip Larkin, immense talent proves a strong deodorant: the petty human personality ends up second, appropriately, to the monumental work. In Riding's case, we are on far less secure ground in the matter of her oeuvre; if she resurfaces as a reputation, it may be in areas less specifically literary and more germane to what her final "language" interests were, vaguely Heideggerian and anticipating (in spirit if not substance) contemporary language theory. She was not really, as Auden called her, "our only living philosophical poet": she renounced her poetry and became a worshiper at another temple. Her new religion was a kind of spiritual linguistics—and in the words of its liturgy, and the liturgy of its words, she was both exonerated and canonized: lone Goddess.

The Habit of Time (or Fleshing Out
the Zeitgeist)

Poems, it is often said, occur outside of time, with such an altered sense of the temporal that experience is released from most of the conventional burdens of chronology. Some poets understand this freedom as a release from all progressive ordering of phenomena within the poem.

Poets recreate time then alter its flow. Time becomes "a" time, which can be stopped or started at will, like a film. Time takes on an almost physical quality; like an element in transformation at an altered temperature, it seems to acquire form.

The *idea* of tenses—the ideas of past, present, future—provides a psychological setting for the poem. If our motion through time is described variously as completed, ongoing, anticipated, then a sense of ourselves forms around each of these *places* in times, not Zeitgeist but *time-flesh*.

The past tense, for example, is used in poetry as much to designate a finished act as to impose the pathos of the irrevocable, the irreversible, and it is from this fixed illusion of defined time that we begin to recount ("Once upon a time . . ."). In Lynn Emanuel's *Hotel Fiesta* (1984) we are almost exclusively in the kingdom of the Past. The rhythms of the poems are those of the remembering mind; the tone is reflective; the tense alternates between the past and variations of present tense set in the past.

From a review of *White Dress,* by Brenda Hillman, *The Long Approach* by Maxine Kumin, and *Hotel Fiesta* by Lynn Emanuel, in *Western Humanities Review* (Winter 1986–87).

For all practical purposes time has stopped in these poems, the drawbridge has been raised, and the order of relationship is totemic: each poet remains in a suspended position, that of child to parent or child to the world of the adult. The great music, the major themes, swell from other lives:

> In her black hat, the one you used to watch
> Through a stammer in the drapes.
> In that small town of cold hotels, you were the girl in the dress,
> Red as a house burning down.
> > (Emanuel, "Of Your Father's Indiscretions
> > and the Train to California," 5)

Stylistically, Emanuel desires to encapsulate time. Her impulse is narrative, to make the act of remembering and imagining one.

> For the first time I could remember
> Grandmother's hair breaking in a fine
>
> Shiver from the braid,
> Her house at the top of the sloped avenue
>
> Below which the world grew small.
> > (Emanuel, "On Returning to Carthage
> > to Excavate an Ancient Sacrificial Site," 39)

This desire to contain time is symptomatic of the strengths of this poet. She has remarkable gifts for reconstructing the past moment; her writing is filled with poignancy and grace. And Zeitfleisch. It is no accident that one of Lynn Emanuel's recurring themes is archaeology, the science of recovering and recreating the past with artifacts and relics of human life. Here is a poem about a husband, an archaeologist, recovering the body of a woman executed centuries earlier for adultery.

> [It]
> Made me think of what we saw in ancient Eglon once:
> A woman buried with her head in her lap, the cure
> For infidelity, the old lust over-ended by the axe.
> My husband worked all one night and in the end

> I think he grew to love her, especially there,
> With the earth on her like a black wing.

("The Dig," 6)

The poem is without rancor, though another kind of "adultery" is taking place: in an astonishing linkage of past and present the husband grows to love the mutilated body of desire, cocooned in time. The "infidelity" moves back and forth along a temporal line that includes the present of the narrator, the past, and the "perfect" past, as he touches the body of the other woman before his wife's eyes. The comprehension of how time "travels" here is extraordinary, and the poem's execution underscores this reflective movement ("Made me think," "I think").

The poet chooses not to employ the present tense to animate this tableau, for a good reason. To think of this poem in the present is to imagine a dramatic failure of *tone*. Why? The poem requires the past's aura of hermetic, charmed space. Further, one of the "psychologies" the present tense embodies is a sense of self-consciousness, and this is a poem in which the self wishes to be effaced, to be like the recovered body, a "present absence," a wife who steps out of time, witnesses but does not judge. The poem is lovely, and it is over. Beauty and desire are *stopped,* the "present" earth lifts off like "a black wing," the pun "over-ended" is inspired, since the dead woman repeats her "ending" in the poem's present.

Poets "invent" a tense and fall in love with it. Further, a particular tense becomes associated with a particular tone: the past is authoritative, if only by virtue of its finality, and the present implies a continuous epiphany, in which the poem measures its effect by how successfully it refuses the mimetic. (The *now* is not *like* anything else.)

Use of the present insures other qualities of rhetorical tone— for example, the mock-ingenuousness of speech appearing to "discover" itself as it is spoken. Here is an example, again from Lynn Emanuel—a poem that appears to be about a father's sexual abuse of his small daughter.

> Her father talks about the divorce.
> Now it is quiet.

Grandmother has left, her tight stockings
Showed rainbows,
And someone's upstairs undressing,
His dog tags making faint noise.
Her father walks into the room.
He is naked and there are certain
Parts of him that are shadows.
And he pulls the blankets to the floor
And then the sheet—as if not to wake her—
And he lifts her up and whispers his wife's name—
Rachel, Rachel
And he takes her hand, small with its clean nails,
And he puts it to the dark:
Oh Rae, Oh Rachel he says
And over his shoulder she can see
The long hall mirror framed in black wood

                                                ("She Is Six," 30)

Here the present tense is used to great advantage within the past, since the poet wishes to make it clear that what happened is unfinished, the moment's confusion and horror ongoing. Its use stops the story—allows the experience to be lived in as well as framed. The present tense allows us to enter the poem's event at the moment of its occurrence. Because we see through the eyes of a child, there is mystery, fear ("Parts of him that are shadows"); there are many questions left unanswered. The closely rendered details of the physical as a child would notice them—things that are odd, that are noisy or hidden—add to the trauma of the narrator. The body takes on aspects of wonder and terror; the child does not see *herself* in the mirror over the father's shoulder; she sees only the mirror, a horrifying image of her own "disappearance," swallowed by the father's body. When the present tense is used in this manner, the past opens to the present, we are allowed to mourn, and the poem is elegiac in tone and lyrical in style—in the precise sense Virginia Woolf meant when she called her novel *To the Lighthouse* elegiac and lyrical. The past is revived; it then becomes the present, expressing emotion directly. Emanuel does this work in the present past brilliantly, in poem after poem.

Information is not transformable; it is self-enclosed, and the self seems alone in time, like a patron in a movie theater or a viewer of a Hopper painting, pure consciousness. Here is Emanuel:

> In L.A. someone is kissing Veronica Lake
> And here, outside the window, the neon says *Hotel Clover.*
> . . . .
> Waltzing slowly in the room, hands on her forehead,
> The sign outside repeating *Clover, Clover, Clover.*
> ("What I Know about the End of the Second World War," 38)

Again, the poet's choice of time dictates style. The nostalgic style requires that the "historical" present tense be another kind of past tense—enclosed, finished. The present is not allowed the self-awareness that it inherently possesses. The self merely reports; its attention is limited entirely to detail, oversymbolized, circumstantial detail. What accrues is a world without questions—and the present is full of questions. With that dread adjective *cinematic*, it imposes "auteur" consciousness on the poem.

Cheer is not a word one would associate with Brenda Hillman's poems. She is writing in that "other" present (or the present of the Other)—that is to say, the lyrical present tense, the oracular, so familiar to us from the work of Louise Glück.

This tense is characterized by its heightened tone; the speaker in the poems is "removed," as with a spiritualist's, or a medium's, removal. In this sense the present tense is like the future—and is tied to no past, a kind of altered mental state. If nostalgia is the stopped past, and if the elegiac (as in the Emanuel "archaeological" poem) is in motion through time, these poems are elegies for the present in the present.

> Night is too full, like remembered birthdays
> When you were supposed to be happy.
> From the seat of honor you could stare
> Into the past with its wretched glitter,
>
> Things that made you what you are,
> As now each star is a separate event
> Marking its section of heaven
> Like an old firefly. If this is the past,

That ring and tinsel,
You are the future, above it, really,
Clutching that gray extension of your eye,
Trying to steady it.

("Telescope," 9)

Here we are, like ruined aristocracy,
Sent out to guard the provinces.
My eyes are worse.
The silver beech, so dead
Before, seems to approach our house.

("In the Provinces," 28)

Pain is an iron flower. I do not fear it:
It surrounds a garden with its long black fences
A garden of sacrifice

Where children are already playing.

("Birth," 46)

Hillman's use of the second person also intensifies the state of the visionary; the "I" is dislocated, impersonalized, Kafka-ized. She sees through familiar things with hallucinatory clarity, speaks with desperation's imperative:

Look at the corner, near the movie house:
See the whore, barelegged, lonely?
Look at the syntax of cars
On the avenue, the racetrack

Like a fine bouquet—is that for you?
Can you enter it?

("Telescope," 9)

Everywhere the mind's eye travels, there is recognition, but not of the *like;* the acknowledgment is of something unfamiliar, unlike, conducting itself in a familiar manner. This tone of "precision angst" would seem to preclude humor, but the poet, in the versatility characteristic of this book, manages it:

We're trapped inside the belly of a horse:
Suddenly survival isn't worth much.
. . . .

And it seems the enemy no longer cares for us.
It seems the enemy is singing songs.

("February," 10)

Hillman refuses the past, refuses, to a large extent, narrative. For her the present tense becomes an opportunity for a lyric that is Rilkean in its ecstasy and despair. She chooses the unsolved mystery of the present, and the choice is to her great advantage. She is a poet who has found the exact *timing* for her voice, and these startling poems are proof.

It is hard to imagine a poet's residing entirely in the future. Still, if the "habit of time" in poems can be viewed in familial terms, if nostalgic poems keep us "children" in the universe and the altered present makes us intellectually current with ourselves (an adulthood)—then where are the Moms and Dads in poetry, and what future are they facing?

In Maxine Kumin's new book, *The Long Approach*, the voice is maternal to the world. Though she is by no means aged, her perspective in these poems is collected and matured; often she speaks parent to child, teacher to student, wise elder to a self-destructive world. Her poems have a Peaceable Kingdom kind of sagesse: she loves the beasts and the birds in the fields, but her love leans to moral allegory; it is teaching love. Nature is not passive, the receptor of pantheism, it too is our instructor. The plants that grow staked to poles, the cultivation of nature, give her a future:

Today I am going up in the sky with these tendrils,
these snakelets that reach, reach, double back and respell . . .
. . . today I am
going up to cross over and seize you, you and the little boy
who belong to us, although at arm's length always.
Down the broad green stem I will bear you home
In the numinous light of late summer to the brown loam.

("Expatriate," 14)

"I am going up" . . . "I will"—the bright echo of resolve would be positively chivalric as well as fairy tale bean stalkish were this poem not so much a fierce and protective maternal gesture. The "will" of the future tense carries this "heroic" tone with natural aplomb.

There are many other mother-protector poems. In one of them her students lie on the grass in the sun, with their "illegal puppies," as the teacher contemplates fate. "Here" she says "everything is hopeful / because unconsidered." *She* is considering the "Poseidon submarine carrying / like the fish, its eggs enough / to flood the pond . . . ," and the maternal image turns ominous; mother-specter, the future turned back on itself, burns a caesura in the sunny air.

Kumin's view of tomorrow is alternately hopeless but giddy with despair ("out there crisping in one another's arms") and calmly defiant. She describes the ritual maiming of the gingko and "thereupon every severed shoot / comes back, takes on / a human form." "This means," she says, "*we are all to be rescued.*" Her future is considered in a garden sense; there is no past for the growing shoot, only movement forward in the present.

So a poem called "Grandchild" is simply about surviving in the moment, on "monkey-wit," a habit of being in time, a lush dreamy poem of the newborn and the mothers:

> I stand at the window
> watching the ancient boundaries that flow
> between my daughter's life and mine dissolve . . .
> and I am a young unsure mother again
> stiffly clutching the twelve-limbed raw
> creature that broke from between my legs . . .
>
> ("Grandchild," 12)

We relearn ourselves in the future—in fact, in a present that pulls both past and future into it:

> This skill comes back
> like learning how to swim. Comes warm and quick
> as first milk in the breasts. I comfort you.
> Body to body my monkey-wit soaks through.
>
> (13)

Her writing is, as always, succinct, quick-eyed, whimsical. And these are poems that refuse to let go of the earth, refuse to give up. _Her present tense, tinged with the future tense's equal components of dread and daring_, offers lessons to the world on our "common human fate." If this sounds grand, it is perhaps an unavoidable style of Kumin's, given her unequivocal, loving embrace of Nature's time.

These are poets of unquestionable skill, whose poems have "located" themselves within tenses, or found a "temporal tone" concomitant with their particular vision; that is to say, their time is their style. There is an oddness in imagining Brenda Hillman writing poems defined by (and within) the past, just as Lynn Emanuel seems full-time resident in experience shaped by past time, unaltered by the flux of the immediate.

In this place of intersection of tense and tone a "traveling present" tense has sprung up, allowing the poem to cut itself free of rhetorical or metaphorical expectations. We read this poem as an associational text in which the lines themselves are emblems of experience and epiphany.

We read this poem as if tense were hierarchical and not declensive; we read this poem, in one sense, as synonymous with "pure lyric," the redress of metaphor.

And we read further, as if to suggest that we are seeking to consult poetry and poets, as oracles, interpreters, who comment cryptically and definitely on our lives as we disappear into time. If there _was_ intelligent life on earth, poetry _is_ the remainder of that design.

The Wild Iris

The world of Louise Glück's poems has always been conventional; her god the God of revelation, the family milieu bourgeois and patriarchal, the sexual ethos unrelievedly Freudian. But Glück's preoccupation with convention stems from a much deeper obsession with order, and with clarification: in her poems a failing world is forced to display its wounds, to pursue its logic to inevitable irrational extreme, to witness its own ambivalence toward and flight from taboo, the frailty of its moral judgments. Convention is taken apart to display pathology—and the poet's role is surgical: "This is mastery," she has said, "whose active mode is dissection."

In poem after poem we see a moral world pinned helplessly to its dilemma of absolutes, rendered unsparingly. Thus, in an early poem inspired by Edvard Munch's painting *The Sick Child*, a mother is admonished for not turning away from her dying little one ("Then it is wrong, wrong / to hold her—"), since death will inevitably make its claim and the surviving children never forget the mother's neglect; thus, in another poem we witness the anorexic child's "need to perfect" her body (which she compares with the poet's need for precision)—"Of which death is the mere byproduct"; and finally, bitterly, a woman's body "*is* a grave; it will accept / anything."

It is clear that it is genius wielding this blade and that it is a double-edged genius: intellectual insights accrue, dazzling and implacable, but the emotions that inspire the poems are disconnected and wrenching, as if a wound (self-inflicted) could speak.

From a review of *The Wild Iris* by Louise Glück, in *American Poetry Review* (January–February 1993).

She resists the trappings of mastery: there are no flourishes, no virtuoso effects in Glück. From her harsh-lit starkness to the weary ascendance of the oracle, we are meant to see that the knife is wielded in service of a higher power. Unlike her literary peers, she offers little evidence of personality (even at her most psycho-anecdotal); rather, she displays the unexpected passions of the zealot. The poet is simply a scribe, vatic translator of divine logos.

It is hardly surprising that there has been, till now, no god capable of withstanding Glück's scrutiny. In her poems perfection has become synonymous with stasis, paralysis, stopped time, morbidity—even as the blade sculpts a new image to fit her protean longing. In *The Triumph of Achilles* the scribe-poets themselves are chastised for the futility of testimony in words; she saves her scorn for "we who would leave behind exact records."

Still, Louise Glück has searched for God even in despair, and in *The Wild Iris* she has found her deity on earth, among the flowers. This book reads like a culmination of a divine quest—from her earliest "possessed voices" (poems from which her famous oracular presence derived) to her ransacking of the Greek pantheon for mythological narrative sufficient to the interrogations of the secular, through Dionysian Christ figures to the Judaic God of Scripture to *Ararat*'s dubious modern messiah, psychoanalysis.

> Do you know what I was, how I lived? You know
> what despair is; then
> winter should have meaning for you.
>
> ("Snowdrops," 6)

Winter, the cold retraction of promise, the cycle of withering and dying, is a clue to a new perspective. Nevertheless, *The Wild Iris* begins on what appears to be familiar Glück ground. There is the title's flirtation with myth: Iris is the rainbow goddess, whose prism-bridge connects sky and earth. The image calls up Wordsworth's fleeting rainbow—coupled with the particular symbology of the visual: the iris of the eye, the mind's entrapment in and by what is *seen*, and botanical reference. In botany the wild, or false, iris, *pseudacorus*, is not cultivated; it grows outside the gardener's borders, thus providing one of the book's central metaphors: undomesticated thriving versus the garden.

The reader struggles to find a locus in these poems—where exactly are we? The poems' structures provide some assistance. They are dialogues (or an eclogue) between the god and/or between a human speaker and the human speaker and blossoms. The time span of the book is one season's flowering, from spring through late autumn. Flowers seem to speak by eerie ventriloquism—the projected voices of deity or poet—but they possess their own pathos. The poet-speaker's voice, waking and sleeping, chimes "Matins" and "Vespers," in the liturgical tradition of The Book of Common Prayer or the Latin Office. Light, dark, morning, evening—maybe we're in the familiar split world of dualism, the Manichaean god who has plagued Glück through many avatars?

> Look at the night sky:
> I have two selves, two kinds of power.
>
> ("Spring Snow," 9)

In fact, Glück is using notions of duality to interrogate a new god—or a newly cast vision of an old god. All of the speaking flowers represent the earth itself, from the garden grown ("The White Rose," "The White Lily") to the insistent voices of weeds and wildflowers, which seem at first to have scattered, opinionated "identities" that reflect human preoccupations. (For example, in a poem called "Ipomoea" the morning glory speaks bitterly about its destiny, having only one day to blossom, then turns its musings, resignedly, to faith.)

But from what, or whom, do these voices derive? Are we meant to see them as subjective meditations of the poet alone, or are they connected to a more obvious theology, mythology? There are hints, in the excited yet removed musical tone of the poems, that we've entered momentousness: some great glory has recently passed from the earth (the shadow of the romantics is as long as God's on this landscape!)—and Glück's inspiration for these poems seems drawn direct from Wordsworth:

> To me the meanest flower that blows can give
> Thoughts that do often lie too deep for tears.
>
> ("Ode on Intimations of Immortality")

The talking flowers here indeed offer "thoughts too deep for tears," and they are meant to impart them as living consciousnesses of the earth. Nature is both inherently alive *and* representative of the soul's subjective animation—the world, Wordsworth says, which we half-perceive and half-create.

This world we half-perceive and half-create links the poems even more strongly to the story of Orpheus and Eurydice—and to Rilke. The following excerpt (from Rilke's note to the Hogarth Press version of the *Sonnets to Orpheus*) both clarifies and enlarges Wordsworth's speculation on the grief of flowers and Glück's own focus:

> Transience everywhere plunges into a deep being. . . . Not into a beyond, the shadow of which darkens the earth, but into a whole, into a *whole*. Nature, the things we move among and use, are provisional and perishable, but, so long as we are here, they are *our* possession and our friendship, sharing the knowledge of our grief and gladness, as they have already been the confidants of our forebears. . . . Transform? Yes; for our task is so deeply and so passionately to impress upon ourselves this provisional and perishable earth, that its essential being will arise again "invisibly" in us.

It is Rilke's vision of the "young dead girl," the one "whose incompletion and innocence holds open the door of the grave, so that she, gone from us, belongs to those powers who keep half of life fresh and open toward the other wound-open half" that drives forward the *Sonnets* and Glück's *Iris*. The dead girl, Eurydice, the poet's "other half," banished to the underworld:

> But you now, dear girl, whom I loved like a flower whose name
> I didn't know, you who so early were taken away:
> I will once more call up your image and show it to them,
> beautiful companion of the unsubduable cry.
> > (Sonnet XXV, trans. Stephen Mitchell)

> you won't hear it in the other world,
> not clearly again,
> not in the birdcall or human cry,

```
              not the clear sound, only
              persistent echoing
              in all sound that means good-bye, good-bye—
                                    ("End of Winter," 10)
```

So we encounter the voice of leave-taking, the voice of the split world of the Orphic myth (what Rilke called the "Double World")—but, despite this built-in lyricism, Glück's voice is at times brutally ironic, rejecting and rejected, outspoken. The voice is Eurydice but is, in fact, Eurydice *risen,* like Persephone, back for the summer, a lot wiser. Rilke may not know the name of a flower, but Glück does; she knows each one by heart. Further, she wishes mightily to distance herself from the merely pastoral:

```
                                                  I am
              at fault, at fault, I asked you
              to be human—I am no needier
              than other people. But the absence
              of all feeling, of the least
              concern for me—I might as well go on
              addressing the birches,
              as in my former life: let them
              do their worst, let them
              bury me with the Romantics,
              their pointed yellow leaves
              falling and covering me.
                                    ("Matins," 13)
```

Furthermore, as she divides her flowers into the cultivated species and the wild blossoms, also recording human preference of light over dark, she intimates the power of one "half" of perception over the other. The conventional sects that look "up" to see God in his heaven (or in disillusioned retreat from all of human creation) have tyrannized the cults that look "down" to the earth—the rational over the emotional, the intellectual over the intuitive, etc., etc.

But surely she has not made it so easy for us? Is this (paraphrased in current critical *reducto-speak*) Apollonian/male/skyish versus Dionysian/female/chthonic? The answer's yes but with an admonition attached:

> No one wants to hear
> impressions of the natural world: you will be
> laughed at again; scorn will be piled on you.
> As for what you're actually
> hearing this morning: think twice
> before you tell anyone what was said in this field
> and by whom.
>
> ("Daisies," 39)

The warning to "think twice" is both a play on the notion of duality and a warning: don't assume too much. The "don't tell anyone" gives her words the power of subversiveness: cloaked figures in the field, clandestine gnomic rituals.

> —O
> the soul! the soul! Is it enough
> only to look inward? Contempt
> for humanity is one thing, but why
> disdain the expansive
> field, your gaze rising over the clear heads
> of the wild buttercups into what? Your poor
> idea of heaven: absence
> of change. Better than earth? How
> would you know, who are neither
> here nor there, standing in our midst?
>
> ("Field Flowers," 28)

To be neither "here nor there" is to be human, split, dichotomized. How to restore these divided parts to the whole?

Stylistically and tonally, *The Wild Iris* has a profound wholeness. Every poem in the book is set up in essentially the same way, and it is a style familiar to Glück's readers. Each poem is a dramatic voice, a declarative lyric, framed in startling apostrophe. The combination of rhetorical and colloquial diction ("Contempt for humanity is one thing") works like a brake of deadpan humor on that high-priestess interrogative tone—as if Rilke were undercut with Auden at his most acerbic.

The poems are accentual/syllabic—rarely more than seven

syllables per line and a strong two-or-three stress line. The pattern creates a hypnotic rhythm, an argument, a complaint, but with a fine carefully worked music:

> doing what you always do,
> mourning and laying blame,
> always the two together.

> ("Witchgrass," 23)

In "Field Flowers" Nature's voice is a scornful one. The "glory" for the flower is not in flowering itself but in the startled awakening of the seed, then seed-split, tropism, the shoot unfurling toward the great light. *Vision* is made a mockery, both the physical act of sight (staring at the horizon) and the *visions,* philosophical and pious, imposed on that eye line. The vault of the sky has created a false belief, a blind cathedral, Orpheus' backward look. Poetic vision, including romantic nature worship, is a joke.

> Not I, you idiot, not self, but we, we—waves
> of sky blue like
> a critique of heaven: why
> do you treasure your voice
> when to be one thing
> is to be next to nothing?
> Why do you look up? To hear
> an echo like the voice
> of god? You are all the same to us,
> solitary, standing above us, planning
> your silly lives.

> ("Scilla," 14)

So much for the Solitary Reaper. So much for the Lyre. Her previous gods have indeed occupied a remote heaven; the sufferings of mortals have been viewed from this exalted position. Glück has always associated earth with death; her recurring glimpses of the "garden" in other books were mortuarial, embalmed—but now she is closer to accepting the death earth represents.

> —I am ashamed
> at what I thought you were,

distant from us, regarding us
as an experiment: it is
a bitter thing to be
the disposable animal,
a bitter thing.

("Matins," 31)

Bitter death lies at the center of *The Wild Iris,* as it does in all her other books. But this is the first time that this bitterness does not cause an injured turning away from the earth. Instead, she moves toward the earth, cutting through all the "lies": the Bible, the Garden, the Adamic myth, Heaven and Hell, the solitary ego of the artist, the anthropomorphic God himself, the human act of making distinctions—that is, language, art, poetry.

Now we stare into a world that has been effectively dismantled, reduced to speaking *object.*

Wordsworth's exhortation, to cast aside the veil of the familiar and *see,* is ultimately heeded. Nature may be God, yes, but the deity no longer has to be named God. Here is a new god, nature, an impersonal force, a collective animator, not so much Wordsworth's "clouds of glory" as the prime force Goethe set forth in his botanical writings: *all is leaf* (or "white light" obscured by matter, as one poem puts it).

But *think twice:* she is moving closer to Blake: Innocence after Experience, she is Eurydice risen. She is Rilke's "essential being" rising again "invisibly" to impart a message:

with a child's fierce confidence of imminent power
preparing to defeat
these weaknesses, to succumb
to nothing, the time directly

prior to flowering, the epoch of mastery

before the appearance of the gift,
before possession.

("The Doorway," 33)

The word *possession* describes exactly the moment in which the psyche splits, becoming both active and passive, as it mirrors itself. The verb *possess* "reads" either way, to be claimed or to claim, sexually or otherwise. And *gift* and *flower* are active verbs as well as things—the poet's eye *and* the object.

It is "prior to flowering" that we give up our mastery, or oneness, and are purchased by a vision of ourselves, our egos, and split into distinctions, fragments, shatter. If mastery's "active mode" is dissection, then this is the body entire prior to fragmentation.

Thus, the outcast's voice, that of weed or wildflower, holds forth in *The Wild Iris*. We've rarely heard the voice of the "other order," outside the "law" of the cultivated. The departing God is male, the Father. Here is the She-God, Demeter, Lilith, Mother Goddess: both wholeness and void.

> Something
> comes into the world unwelcome
> calling disorder, disorder—
>
> ("Witchgrass," 22)

In "Witchgrass" the defiant voice of the weed precedes a quick portrait of a man and a woman, a husband and wife, lying in bed (one of the few "peopled" moments in the poems), wrapped in the bleakness of diminished passion.

> what you see happening
> right here in this bed,
> a little paradigm
> of failure. One of your precious flowers
> dies here almost every day
> and you can't rest until
> you attack the cause, meaning
> whatever is left.
>
> ("Witchgrass," 22–23)

It's just another way "to blame one tribe for everything—as we both know / if you worship one god, you only need / one enemy—I'm not the enemy." Earth, witchgrass, witch, woman—the blamed tribe, not the enemy. Rather, what she describes is another kind of mastery, whose *passive* mode is potential, maternality, the fertile field.

> I don't need your praise
> to survive. I was here first,
> before you were here, before
> you ever planted a garden.
> And I'll be here when only the sun and moon
> are left, and the sea, and the wide field.
>
> I will constitute the field.
>
> > ("Witchgrass," 23)

The authority of that last line rings through the book—joined with *all things prior to flowering*. If a woman's body *is* a grave, then surely we have here, if not a reversal of that slur, a revision of it—in order to readjust our sight, Orpheus' backward sight. Indeed, a grave will accept anything, but it is as earth, which accepts and turns death to life.

Thus, the book's final image begins as a portrait of burial but becomes a figure planting a bulb, a "dead" life.

> I felt your two hands
> bury me to release its splendor.
>
> > ("The White Lilies," 63)

"During this one summer we have entered eternity," she says to her Orphic companion, and we are returned to the beginning of the book, with its powerful hint of birth and rebirth:

> You who do not remember
> passage from the other world
> I tell you I could speak again: whatever
> returns from oblivion returns
> to find a voice.
>
> > ("The Wild Iris," 1)

Returning to the book's first poem, the title poem, we find an extraordinary Rilkean image of a fountain pouring up from the center of "my life" and praise deep "blues" of the flower. To die with the flowers, to recast oblivion, is—dare we use this word regarding Glück?—an image of *hope*. If this is not credible to her readers, perhaps it is enough to think of her as earthbound, chthonic, but not imprisoned. Eurydice-with-a-blade will constitute the field.

Breaking Out of the Genre Ghetto

For Teresa McKenna and Michelle Latiolais

Why do most American graduate writing programs ghettoize poetry and fiction? Why do poets and fiction writers support this isolationism? It's obvious that poetry and fiction are different genres, but why should this lead to specialized education and aesthetic suspicion, literary territoriality akin to gang partition: Blood turf, Crip turf? Why, in my early years as a writer in New York City, did my poet friends label fiction writers "word-creepers" (a term corrupted from Roethke) and novelists scorn poets as "word-wankers"? (Or was it the other way around?) Or did I just make up this "poetic" notion that the Word itself is split into active discourse and ecstatic meditation?

These questions are not meant to be rhetorical. There are a variety of answers—the "us and them" politics of American culture, that something in us that really does love a wall, a fence, a line drawn in the sand; something anti-intellectual that casts a suspicious eye on the "generalist" (a term that has become a disdainful epithet in academic circles on a par with *liberal* in politics). Knowledge and expertise in many areas lead to charges of dilettantism or hybridism, as if ability in one field is diluted or compromised by accomplishment in another.

Paideuma, Pound reminds us, is a complex of ideas conditioning a people's views of themselves at a given epoch in history. Today the conventional wisdom is that poetry is lyrical; fiction is narrative. Poetry is elliptical; fiction, linear. Poetry is hermetic;

From reviews of three books by Rita Dove: *Through the Ivory Gate, Selected Poems,* and *Fifth Sunday,* and three books by Sandra Cisneros: *Loose Woman, The House on Mango Street,* and *Woman Hollering Creek and Other Stories,* in *Parnassus* 20, nos. 1–2 (1995).

fiction, transactive. And oh, yes—fiction has an audience; poetry doesn't. Then, too, both genres take a defensive position vis-à-vis the Academy and its current posse of Muse-Busters, critical theorists who refuse to distinguish between an epic and a laundry list as "texts." This Academy Rag is enough to push the contenders back in their corners forever.

Nobody wants to force poetry and fiction into a shotgun marriage. But there are signs that the bias against writers who "cross-voice" has diminished. (Cross-voicing is like cross-dressing, only the author usually doesn't get credit for her daring fashion sense.) Rita Dove and Sandra Cisneros, among others,* have published poetry and fiction—whether in opposition, or indifference, to literary purdah, I can't say. Rita Dove is among our most committed genre benders. A few years ago, at a Vanderbilt University conference on "Poets Who Write Fiction," she spoke with gentle incredulity about the American habit of segregating the genres, like rich and poor neighborhoods. She'd grown up reading and loving both fiction and poetry, unaware of any lurking danger of dabbling. Then she'd won a Fulbright to Germany, where she matured as a writer and where "poets write plays, novelists compose libretti, playwrights write novels—they would not understand our restrictiveness."

There's no sense of this "restrictiveness" in Dove's work. Her *Selected Poems* offers many examples of what William Walsh called "lyric narrative," her edgy blend of plot and distilled music. The notion of lyric narrative isn't new. There are many poets besides Dove whose lyric music flows around islands of charged detail within a poem. These islands, or stepping stones, accrue into a narrative that sparkles and momentarily dams the lyric stream then releases it again.

Consider these lines from "Nigger Song: An Odyssey":

> We six pile in, the engine churning ink
> We ride into the night.

---

*Others like Michael Ondaatje, Mary Karr, Kelly Cherry, Denis Johnson, Adrian C. Lewis, Stephen Dobyns, Maura Stanton, Quincey, Troupe, and, from another generation, Mark Strand come to mind—but space is limited.

Past factories, past graveyards
And the broken eyes of windows, we ride
Into the gray-green nigger night.

Or these lines from "The Zeppelin Factory" in *Thomas and Beulah:*

The zeppelin factory
needed workers all right—
but standing in the cage
of the whale's belly, sparks
flying off the joints
and noise thundering,
Thomas wanted to sit
right down and cry.

In "Nigger Song" the repetitions "We ride" . . . "we ride,"
"past" . . . "past" (playing on the passage of time and *passed*), and
"night" . . . "night" (with its related near-rhymes *pile* and *eyes*)
slow down the narrative for lyric effect. The atmosphere is like a
slow-motion speeding dream. In "The Zeppelin Factory" Thomas
is a latter-day Jonah: the cage of the whale's belly reinforces
Thomas's claustrophobia and hopelessness; the sound of his beat-
ing heart in *its* cage is drowned out by the thundering noise of the
machinery. This job is a trap: a coffin, death's gigantic waiting
room.

Though undeniably prose, the following passage from Dove's
novel *Through the Ivory Gate* also treats lyric narrative as an exten-
sion of poetic rhythm:

Virginia never paid attention . . . preferring to gaze through
the glass from the backseat at the glittering slashes of light escap-
ing from the coated windowpanes cracked open for air, and the
grey-streaked smoke that billowed from grates and chimneys and
hung at shoulder level like lost thunderclouds. What function
had he performed among the reeking tiers of this manmade
purgatory, how had his efforts born fruit or withered among the
smoking terraces of Babel, how was it that he couldn't resist the
compulsion to return to the scene of his daily humiliations on his
day off, circling his place of labor like a dog following the scent
of its mother back to the house from which he'd been sold?

With the rising-falling cadences of the jeremiad, the sermon, and the hymn, this passage achieves the stylistic gloss that signals poetry-in-prose. The stresses of *labor, mother,* and *been sold* drive a hard rhythmic bargain (the speaker's telling us something irresistible). As the narrative music reaches the crescendo and diminuendo of the conclusion, the words lift off into poetry (or prose poetry) and the lyric builds to an emotional pitch: the daughter's agitation as she views the scene of her father's "daily humiliations" is dramatized by the blunt adjective next to the mocking singsong of the polysyllabic noun. Dove's prose is luxurious, its long rolling rhythms and its clauses and phrases welling up then overflowing. The momentum surges and subsides. Her poems, however, are spare, sculpted yet *charged*. She pares the narrative down until it is a skeletal map of cadence, an intimation of sequence at the heart of the lyric cry.

Reading "Thomas wanted to sit / right down and cry" and "back to the house from which he'd been sold" in context makes us conscious of how the mind organizes rhythm and diction in response to a *tilt,* an adjustment of the driver's seat and the windshield and rearview mirrors of genre. "Thomas wanted to sit / right down and cry" is not so much the culmination of a rhythmic pattern as a relinquishing of rhythm that mimics the monotony of the dead-end job. The image of a grown man breaking down and crying in the middle of a factory is as unexpected as a blues riff; it follows no sequence, blocks the pathway of linear thought. "Back to the house from which he'd been sold," by contrast, demands a full rhythmic exploration, all the stops pulled out. It's the climax of a direct, linear buildup.

Dove's syntactical "shaping," what Helen Vendler calls her "pure shapes," is much in evidence in *Selected Poems.* The poems in *The Yellow House on the Corner* (her first book) are accomplished but confected in what Dove has called a "hodgepodge" of styles. By *Museum* (1983) she has begun to flex her muscles. *Thomas and Beulah,* the last book in the triptych of her *Selected Poems,* is her most fully realized work. A narrative cycle of poems based on the lives of her grandparents in Akron, Ohio, *Thomas and Beulah,* as Dove puts it, undeniably "tells two sides of a story and [is] meant to be read in sequence." But there's a crucial absence: what is left unsaid by the book's omniscient speaker acts as a counterpoint to the main harmonies, so that the reader becomes a silent narrator, reading between the lines of plot and eavesdropping on the characters' voices and thoughts about courtship, marriage, children, work, death. Dove is rarely discursive.

If the overall drive of Dove's poems is lyrical, their cumulative effect is narrative. "Summit Beach," a set piece that has obsessed Dove since she first sketched it, is a fine example of genre tailoring and thrifty recycling. Recounted first in *Fifth Sunday* (1985), a collection of short stories, reworked as poems in both *Thomas and Beulah* and *Grace Notes* then resurrected in her novel *Through the Ivory Gate* (1992), it details the circumstances of her grandparents' first meeting at Summit Lake in Akron in 1921.

In "Secondhand Man," a story in *Fifth Sunday,* we're told how Virginia, the grandmother, meets her future husband:

> She'd met him out at Summit Beach one day. In the Twenties, that was the place to go on hot summer days! Clean yellow sand all around the lake, and an amusement park that ran from morning to midnight. She went there with a couple of girlfriends. . . . "High time," everyone used to say to her, but she'd just lift her head and go on about her business. She weren't going to marry just any old Negro. He had to be perfect.
>
> Then she saw James. He'd just come up from Tennessee, working his way up on the riverboats. Folks said his best friend had been lynched down there and he turned his back on the town and said he was never coming back. Well, when she saw this cute little man in a straw hat and a twelve-string guitar under his arm, she got a little flustered. Her girlfriends whispered around to find out who he was, but she acted like she didn't even see him.
>
> He was the hit of Summit Beach. Played that twelve-string guitar like a devil. They'd take off their shoes and sit on the beach toward evening. All the girls loved James. "Oh Jimmy," they'd squeal, "play us a looove song!" He'd laugh and pick out a tune.

In *Through the Ivory Gate* the grandmother tells this incident to her granddaughter. After a verbatim description of Summit Beach as in the previous excerpts, *only in the first person,* Dove adds: "Then I saw your granddaddy. He'd just come up from

Tennessee. Folks said his best friend had been lynched down there and he turned his back on the town," etc.

Both short story and novel are fast-paced, direct recountings of How They Met, filled with vivid, compact detail. The story version is journalistic. James/Thomas becomes a mythic figure, like Apollo, playing his mandolin or guitar, offering sweet music offering *himself*, shaking up and reordering the familiar. The second version of the anecdote takes on the excited, voluble tone of a woman falling in love, whose memory draws the reader into sympathy with the dashing James, who has fled his past and its racist horrors. Dove sets James's riff against the background music of the young ladies oohing and aahing.

What happens in three paragraphs of prose is divided into four separate poems. Let us consider two—first, "Jiving," from *Thomas and Beulah:*

> Heading North, straw hat
> cocked on the back of his head,
>
> . . . He landed
> in Akron, Ohio
> 1921,
>
> on the dingy beach
> of a man-made lake.
>
> Since what he's been through
> he was always jiving, gold hoop
>
> from the right ear jiggling
> a glass stud, bright blue
>
> in his left. The young ladies
> saying *He sure plays*
>
> *that tater bug*
> *like the devil!*

From the earlier prose anecdote, "Jiving" selects straw hat, journey North, and segregated beach, stretching time and slowing the velocity until the tempo picks up with Thomas's (James's) suave, devilish entrance. The twelve-string guitar has changed into a mandolin (the colloquial "tater-bug") and the eye-catching earrings, the pierced lobes once held open by mandolin strings, flash below the straw hat. But the narrator who shades the telling toward Thomas's feelings darkens the mood (the yellow beach is now "dingy") and cunningly spins its psychology. The figure of Thomas/James as a fugitive hero, sexual and renegade, and the image of Virginia/Beulah as the willful golden girl, the barely attainable prize, along with the jaunty rhythms and the couplets that please the reader's sense of symmetry, *add up:* the coupling of two odd spirits.

In "Summit Beach, 1921" (*Grace Notes*) Dove shifts point of view like a novelist so as to deliver a paean to Beulah/Virginia:

> The Negro beach jumped to the twitch
> of an oil drum tattoo and a mandolin . . .
>
> She sat by the fire . . .
>   . . . She was cold,
> thank you, she did not care to dance—
> . . . .
> She could wait, she was gold.
> When the right man smiled it would be
> music skittering up her calf
>
> like a chuckle. She could feel
> the breeze in her ears like water,
> like the air as a child when
> she climbed Papa's shed and stepped off into blue.
>
> with her parasol and invisible wings.

This is an affecting portrait of the grandmother as a headstrong beauty: genteel, if a bit coquettish, yet tough-minded about her prospects. This version strays the most from the original story. Thomas appears only as the phrase "music skittering up her calf" (an insinuating sexual movement). Beulah herself is cold, which soon chimes in gold—extremely valuable and unmeltable except at high temperatures. Yet in the heat of emotion and fantasy, she'd walk off a roof, a daredevil like Thomas, into thin air, still carrying her parasol of self-composure. The lines of "Summit Beach, 1921" are longer and more expansive than those of "Jiving," their ring of inevitability, as if told in the future, tolling from a memory unclouded and fond. The first stanza speaks with the authority of history gathered into the voice of personal experience.

Dove's poetic ambitions may be summed up in these lines from "Ars Poetica" (*Grace Notes*):

> What if I want in this poem to be small,
> a ghost town
> in the larger map of wills.
> Then you can pencil me in as a hawk:
> a traveling x-marks-the-spot.

That "traveling x-marks-the-spot," which diminishes or expands, refusing to be static or fixed, calmly adjusts to the larger demands and identity of language itself. Dove occasionally suffers lapses in concentration, and she can be guilty of imprecise phrasing, but she is never dull or predictable. She is protean. And, despite her mercurial shifts, Dove is in control. She is a mature poet experimenting with form and crossing all borders, sporting embassy plates.

Sandra Cisneros, by contrast, travels without any compass or passport: by stowaway, bootleg, take-no-prisoners, street-smart intuition. Her forays into poetry from prose and back again seem utterly spontaneous, even volatile, a rose-in-the-teeth passion refashioned to contemporary taste. Cherríe Moraga describes Cisneros's poetry as "a kind of international graffiti"— and Cisneros sometimes reads like literary "tagging" (as we say in Los Angeles) or a send-up of Creeley lost in the barrio:

> my crazy
> friend Pat
> boasts she can chug
> one bottle of Pabst
> down one swig
> without even touching . . .
>
> everyone watching
> boy that crazy
> act every time gets them
> bartender runs over

> says lady don't
> do that again
> ("In a redneck bar down the street")

The syntax here is pummeled by the line breaks. The poem lurches, elbows in and out of regular rhythm, stop-and-go like overheard snatches of conversation along a noisy bar. And check out the homegirl cadences of a Chicana facing down rednecks on their own turf, drinking "macho" and chugging it down cold, freaking out the Anglos.

"Little Clown, My Heart" (from *Loose Woman*, Cisneros's most recent book of poems) reads as if it could have been scrawled by e. e. cummings and Lorca on a bender together:

> Little gimp-footed hurray,
> Paper parasol of pleasures,
> Fleshy undertongue of sorrows,
> Sweet potato plant of my addictions,
>
> Acapulco cliff-diver corazon,
> Fine as an obsidian dagger,
> Alley-oop and here we go
> Into the froth, my life,
> Into the flames!

It would be challenging—and exhausting—to explore the poetic influences on Cisneros's spirited temperament: Lorca, Neruda, García Márquez, Gloria Fuertes, Lorna Dee Cervantes, Jimmy Santiago Baca, Plath, and Sexton, the Nuyorican poets. Her pen is also haunted by Cantinflas and the famous Argentinian tango singer Gardel, Mary Cassatt, La Llorona, Zapata—a chorus of talking ghosts jostling for space in her work and waiting to be recast in revisions of myth and history.

Cisneros's zigzags between poetry and fiction mark her profound disregard for the conventional literary career. They also raise other questions: which genre does she favor? which is the stronger impulse? Unlike Dove, whose lyric narratives sing, Cisneros fervently spins dramatic narratives. In both poetry and fiction she creates personae: speakers of verse or prose monologues.

The stories read like long soliloquies, dense and startlingly musical. The poems are anecdotes, fragments, billets-doux, bold cabaret, like the following preface to *My Wicked Wicked Ways:*

> Gentlemen, ladies. If you please—these
> are my wicked poems from when,
> the girl grief decade. My wicked nun
> years, so to speak. I sinned.
> . . . .
> My first felony—I took up with poetry,
> . . . .
> Wife? A woman like me
> whose choice was rolling pin or factory.
> An absurd vice, this wicked wanton
> writer's life.

The "wicked poems" accent the hard choice that becoming a writer represents for a good Chicana daughter. Becoming a writer feels like the sin of pride—striking out alone, independent, ignoring the past and the preordained future. The community's expectation that she will marry or work makes her sin even graver: she is "sentencing" herself to solitary confinement and a life of misunderstanding. The strutting of this Writer's Manifesto is the stylistic prototype for nearly all of Cisneros's poems: sassy, self-pitying, plangent, syncopated, and, as in the following, repetitive:

> It's always the same.
> No liquor in the house.
>
> The last cigar stuffed in its ashes.
> And a heavy dose of poems.
> > ("After Everything")

> The stray lovers
> have gone home.
> The house is cold.
> There is nothing on TV.
> She must write poems.
> > ("The Poet Reflects on Her Solitary Fate")

While her poems glitter with pastiche, flip *pensées,* cracker-jacks, and *churros,* her prose fiction is stylistically more seductive. Bitter pathos and longing run through the words of Esperanza Cordero:

> She says, I am the great great grand cousin of the queen of France. She lives upstairs, over there, next door to Joe the baby-grabber. Keep away from him, she says. He is full of danger. Benny and Bianca own the corner store. They're okay except don't lean on the candy counter. Two girls raggedy as rats live across the street. You don't want to know them. Edna is the lady who owns the building next to you. She used to own a building big as a whale, but her brother sold it. Their mother said, no, no, don't ever sell it. I won't. And then she closed her eyes and he sold it. Alicia is stuck-up ever since she went to college. She used to like me but now she doesn't.
>
> *(The House on Mango Street)*

Cisneros's "Portrait of the Artist as a Young Chicana" is a poignant biography of a young writer. The gamble that Cisneros takes with the form (brief voice vignettes) pays off. Like a haiku, each vignette distills an emotion and sets it in a season of the young girl's development. I've seen *Mango Street* performed as a play, and what the performance confirmed was how perfectly pitched these voices are; they resonate long after we look up from the page. There's no doubt in my mind that Cisneros is a playwright and these voices are dramatic personae.

From *The House on Mango Street* Cisneros moves confidently into *Woman Hollering Creek,* her most mature work, which is connected to the tale of La Llorana, the Weeping Woman. There are many variations on this myth in Central American and Latino/a folklore, grafted onto an Aztec legend of a goddess who cries at night. She is a witchlike apparition who has lost her children (perhaps drowning them in response to her husband's philandering) and seeks them in wailing distress. Children fear her, as do men, especially drunkards, whom she seeks to harm. Haunting streams and creeks and city rivers at night, she paralyzes her victims with fear. Cisneros's version, however, turns La Llorana into a big loud woman—a shouter, a hollerer, an assertive voice. Her wailing becomes a feminist bellow, reversing the image of predatory loss.

In the title story Cleófilas Enriqueta DeLeón Hernández is given in marriage by her father, Don Serafín, to Juan Pedro Martínez Sánchez. Her father tells her on her wedding day that, although her new husband will take her to a town *en el otro lado* (across the border), she will always be welcome to come home. "I am your father, I will never abandon you," he says. This semi-ominous beginning sets the tone, and Cleófilas soon finds herself the prisoner of a brutish husband. Pregnant with her second child, the terrified Cleófilas decides to escape. She puts herself in the hands of a sympathetic nurse and pals, who appear shockingly independent to the sheltered Cleófilas:

> But when they drove across the *arroyo,* the driver opened her mouth and let out a yell as loud as any mariachi. Which startled not only Cleófilas, but Juan Pedrito as well.
> *Pues,* look how cute. I scared you two, right? Sorry. Should've warned you. Every time I cross that bridge I do that. Because of the name, you know. Woman Hollering. *Pues,* I holler. She said this in Spanish pocked with English and laughed. Did you ever notice, Felice continued; how nothing around here is named after a woman? Really. Unless she's the Virgin. I guess you're only famous if you're a virgin. She was laughing again.
> That's why I like the name of that *arroyo.* Makes you want to holler like Tarzan, right?

The heroines of Cisneros's books are all hollerers. An intriguing, motley blend of hard-drinking bitches who screw other women's husbands and talk nasty and various refined souls (many have solid-gold hearts and even write poetry), these women walk through walls. No boundary, no border, can contain them. Neither conventional feminists nor good citizens of any tradition, they always defy expectation. When they wrest free a gun, they shoot to kill.

The most electrifying and eloquent female narrator in *Women Hollering Creek* is Inés Alfaro, long-suffering wife of *el gran general* Emiliano Zapata at the close of the Mexican civil war. Describing the night she learns to leave her body and fly (a Márquezian touch), the language soars into prose poetry:

It was the season of rain. Plum . . . plum plum. All night I listened to that broken string of pearls, bead upon bead upon bead rolling across the waxy leaves of my heart.

I lived with the heartsickness inside me, Miliano, as if the days to come did not exist. And when it seemed the grief would not let me go, I wrapped one of your handkerchiefs around a dried hummingbird, went to the river, whispered, *Virgencita, ayúdame*, kissed it, then tossed the bundle into the waters where it disappeared for a moment before floating downstream in a dizzy swirl of foam.

("Eyes of Zapata")

It's exhilarating to read prose so fiercely elegaic. The words flow effortlessly—*plum, plum, plum* and *bead upon bead upon bead* and *Virgencita, ayúdame*—the words reverberating like the strings of a guitar, the narrator's voice, confiding and throaty, like a *fado* singer's. Markedly influenced by Latin American writing—the dark vitality of the pre-Columbian, contemporary magic realism, Gongora and the Spanish Baroque, Rubén Dario and Sor Juana—Cisneros merges the secret voice of the heart, the voice of Spain, and that of the mestizo:

One night over *milpas* and beyond the *tlacolol*, over *barrancas* and thorny scrub forests, past the thatch roofs of the *jacales* and the stream where the women do the wash, beyond bright bougainvillea, high above canyons and across fields of rice and corn, I flew. The gawky stalks of banana trees swayed beneath me. I saw rivers of cold water and a river of water so bitter they say it flows from the sea. I didn't stop until I reached a grove of high laurels rustling in the center of a town square where all the whitewashed houses shone blue as abalone under the full moon. And I remember my wings were blue and soundless as the wings of a *tecolote*.

("Eyes of Zapata")

The power of this passage can never be paraphrased: its blending of the beautiful Spanish/mestizo words—*tlacolol, barranca, tecolote*—with the soaring and dipping flight of English, the ecstatic trance of the voice and its eerie blue peace, the eloquent *silence* of the altitude, the moving wings. This is poetry.

Cisneros speaks poetry naturally, but her prose sings. Though we build into our aesthetic consciousness a hierarchical view of language—Octavio Paz, for instance, crowns poetic utterance as the essential human expression—surely "poetic utterance" is a cross-voice. It's true that prose is often separated from rhythm by the requirements of conceptual argument. But it's also true, as Paz himself admits, that "at the heart of all prose . . . circulates the invisible rhythmic current."

Rhythm undergirds both lyric and dramatic narrative, and, as these two rhythmic constructs inform style, so language releases its allegiances to genre. Thus, it makes sense to teach rhythmic forms as they occur in all genres, following the path of that invisible current, the primary emblem of time flowing through words. A sensibility as polymorphous, a talent as multifaceted, as Cisneros's urges us to reexamine our aesthetic biases.

It has been crucial for Dove and Cisneros to ignore borders, to cross-pollinate genres. The symbolist dreams of Rubén Dario speak to what I've been saying here: "I pursue a form that my style does not find—and all I encounter is the word that flees . . . and the neck of the great white swan that interrogates me." We've all been interrogated by that great white swan—in our deepest instinctual dreams as writers, somewhere far below genre.

Carolyn Kizer, Superkid

Reviewing children's books not long ago in the *New York Times Book Review,* Carolyn Kizer quoted a favorite childhood "poem," a nonsense ditty by Gertrude Stein:

> Be cool inside the mule
> Be cool inside the mule

She described walking along and saying the lines over and over to herself, having no other awareness of the rhyme than its aural pleasures, the incantatory sound of the words themselves. The words are indeed lulling, but the diction is subversive of "sense"; it is the mantra of a child who is very aware of conventional rhythms but (like the literary renegade who wrote the words) supremely disinterested in imposing convention on thought.

Gertrude Stein, master of this lovely sedition process, stayed in touch with the child's desire to hang on to a language not preempted by logic. Children love rhyme, but love of rhyme merely indicates a delight in repetition; it does not presume a conventionally organized sensibility. Nonsense rhymes delight in their overthrow of syntactical hierarchies, even natural sequence: up is down and left is right; pigs fly, and it is cool inside the mule.

I'd like to take a look at a poem by the grownup Carolyn Kizer written in the sensibility, if not the voice, of the child (ergo the poet)—all-observing, anarchical, word intoxicated.

From *An Answering Music: On the Poetry of Carolyn Kizer* edited by David Rigsbee (Ford-Brown, 1990).

The poem is "The Intruder," recently collected in *Mermaids in the Basement*, and it begins with a long litany of unorthodox delights:

> Dove-note, bone marrow, deer dung,
> Frog's belly distended with finny young,
> Leaf-mould wilderness, harebell, toadstool,
> Odd small snakes roving through the leaves.

Beyond its echo of *Macbeth*'s three witches, brewing up trouble, it has the feel of Vergilian hexameters, long ten- or eleven-syllable lines; it feels Sapphic, with its heavy trochaic and dactylic accents. The result is a poem that is the structural opposite of Stein's: quirky, irregular, authoritative rhythms combined with a nearly courtroom logic.

At first the irregular rhythms seem to underscore an offbeat maternal love, but further study yields a suggestion of underlying contradiction: the mother's much-vaunted unconventionality is shown up for what it in fact is. The poem is finally one of real and chilling epiphany, the remains of a dead bat on the floor and the corpse of her mother's hypocritical "pity."

> Wild and natural!—flashed out her instinctive love, and quick, she
> Picked up the fluttering, bleeding bat the cat laid at her feet,
> And held the little horror to the mirror, where
> He gazed on himself, and shrieked like an old screen door far off.

The mother holding the wounded bat makes a bold, oddly coquettish figure ("Depended from her pinched thumb, each wing"), and her murmured words, "It's rather sweet," clinch the self-regarding sentimentality of her gesture. It is only when the mother sees the lice, "pallid, yellow / nested within the wing-pits" that the tone alters significantly. The reader can hear the mocking echo of the poem's beginning, the Diana-like striding-through-the-forest litany in "pallid, yellow / nested within the wing-pits," and the denouement comes as "the thing dropped from her hands" to be devoured by the unselfconscious cat. The mother, left standing by the puddle of dark blood on the floor, stands now in a harsher light, recognized by her child as victim of her own "tender, wounding passion" for a "whole wild, lost, betrayed and secret life."

The child's loyalties never desert the mother; they alter, rather, with sudden enlightenment, perceiving the enemy: "benevolence, alien / as our clumsy traps"—and the reader feels the wild daughter chaffing in that same snare of love and vanity.

The mother still appears attractive, if now slightly ludicrous; we watch her as she sweeps the kitchen. "Turning on the tap, / She washed and washed the pity from her hands." The terrible word *pity* burns like acid on the mother's hands. Again, in a *Macbeth* echo, the stained hands are held up as dramatic symbols. The irregular meters have rolled over and transformed, like the child's consciousness of the mother, into a more conventional stance. Indeed, the mother is "put in her place" by the return to straightforward iambic pentameter.

She is not wild, after all; she is completely civilized, a mother appreciative of the pathos of nature, though she is finally caught red-handed feeling pity, that most condescending of virtues: "She washed and washed the pity from her hands."

The daughter, however, *is* wild. Her sympathies are forever among the dens and burrows, "whose denizens can turn upon the world / with spitting tongue, an odor, talon, claw." She has thought much further than the mother, even at a tender age, into natural "politics," and the wounded bat and the cat make sense to her in a way that is innate, in the same way the joyous anarchic "cool inside the mule" makes sense. The daughter is a poet and not one afflicted by the pathetic fallacy. Her respect for the mysteries and contradictions of nature, of people and language, is already in place. It is clear that in this mind nothing can be imposed willfully on the world from above: the world must be lived in at all levels, without care for "sting or soil."

It is this sensibility, represented here as a child's, that I find most typical of Carolyn Kizer's worldview. "Cool inside the mule" and this refusal to look away from the bleeding bat signal a kind of tonic imagination always riveted in the actual. As she says in "Pro Femina" (about women): "As we forgive Strindberg and Nietzsche, we forgive all those / Who cannot forget us. We *are* hyenas. Yes, we admit it." Or: "What pomegranate raised you from the dead, / Springing, full-grown, from your own head, Athena!"

There is a childlike delight in the natural outrageousness and a "sagesse" that is close to primitive wisdom—and, finally, an all-embracing love of the world frankly and unapologetically without pity.

Short Reviews

Oppressed by Narrative

With *Telling Women's Lives* Linda Wagner-Martin erects a shaky platform from which to leap headlong into the swirling waters of controversy engulfing the genre of biography. Here's a sample quotation from her introduction:

> The lives of real people have always been more interesting than stories about fictional characters; we may temporarily believe in the exploits of imaginary human beings, but biography wears better.

That will come as news to those of us permanently obsessed with Anna Karenina, Sula, or Holden Caulfield. In light of this quick dispatch of imaginative writing, it is particularly ironic that Ms. Wagner-Martin's overall premise is deeply indebted to fiction, its structures and strategies. These she borrows at will to document the routine "fictionalization" process that occurs in biography; thus she comes up with the rather familiar conclusion that biographies are inventions, as are (to the extent that the impulse to render character is innately speculative) the subjects of biography.

This thinking would seem to reduce biography to the level of second-class creative writing and contradict her own initial division of the two genres. But Ms. Wagner-Martin, a professor of English and comparative literature at the University of North Carolina who is herself a biographer—and one who, in 1987, after publication of "Sylvia Plath: A Biography," was caught in the inevitable commotion surrounding Plath—has bigger conflicts in mind. Ms. Wagner-Martin soon moves away from analysis of biography as fiction and begins to psychoanalyze the genre itself. It is about "conceptualization," she says, it is the "enactment of cultural performance," and, just as the self in everyday life constructs the appearance of a consistent identity, so the biographer must represent that manufactured self whole.

The biographer, Ms. Wagner-Martin says, must decide if the performance self that the real self projects is credible. The biographer then constructs a narrative, either supporting or refuting this performance self. The traditional biographer has a difficult time with life stories of women because, she says, "few women—even women like Eleanor Roosevelt—live public lives" or possess well-developed performance selves. And further: "Harder to discover, private events may be ones purposely kept secret by the subject (such as sexual abuse, dislike for parents, dislike by parents or other unfortunate childhood or adolescent happenings)."

The neglect of women and their stories is tragic and irrefutable; what is questionable is Ms. Wagner-Martin's certainty that there is a particular kind of life story unique to women. Narrative itself is her enemy. She does not believe that women's experience fits neatly into a linear arrangement. And, she says, critics are only looking for the performance narrative to praise: "When the biographer fails to meet the most traditional of biography's rules—to provide a structure of external event as a setting for the subject's life story—critics are disgruntled."

She includes among the disgruntled William H. Pritchard, whose review in the *New York Times Book Review* of Ann Hulbert's *Interior Castle* (a 1992 biography of Jean Stafford) reveals his attempt, she says, to "put biography back into a more traditional mode." In the passage she quotes Mr. Pritchard warns that probing a "subject's childhood, sexual and domestic conflicts, obsessions and compulsions" should not be mistaken for better understanding: "In fact, the more fully we become acquainted with people—in real life or in biography—the more ultimately mysterious and unfathomable they may become."

This passage could not make clearer the argument between

Ms. Wagner-Martin and what she calls traditional critics. Mr. Pritchard is not, in her view, raising questions about how we interpret human experience; rather, he is attempting to repress and restrict real-self stories of women's lives. It becomes clear that, for her, the revelation of repressed detail qualifies as the unprejudiced examination of interior life. She is unlike Janet Malcolm, who in *The Silent Woman,* her new book on Sylvia Plath, Ted Hughes, and their biographers, finds the task of determining individual motive largely elusive, and moves farther *inward,* into questions of how the biographer is both seduced and repelled by her subject, eventually wondering what purpose biography finally serves. Ms. Wagner-Martin moves outward into cultural analysis.

She has no serious questions about the impossibility of one human being rendering another's life story whole and accessible within language. Rather, she has answers for readers and writers alike, providing, oddly, her own performance narrative. Here it is: the reason there are not many, or many effective, biographies of women is the failure of the genre itself, as conceived and executed by men—and by women who attempt to tell women's life stories in "traditional" form—and as bolstered by critics. These restrictions have made the correct recounting of women's lives unlikely.

But Ms. Wagner-Martin sees hope in "new ways," which include structures "dependent less on chronology than on 'moments of being.' " She does not, however, provide many examples from biography, drawing instead on the use of "recognizable voice" in fiction, memoir, and autobiography by women.

Presumably, once these new ways are firmly in place, all women will live happily ever after, at least within the confines of Reconstituted Biography. At least, that's the way the story is supposed to go. *Middlemarch,* anyone?

Doorkeepers of the Heart

Who was the very first author in the world? The answer, Jane Hirshfield says in her adventurous anthology, *Women in Praise of the Sacred: Forty-three Centuries of Spiritual Poetry by Women,* is Enheduanna, a Sumerian high priestess who around 2300 B.C., inscribed her hymns to the moon goddess on cuneiform tablets:

> You thunder in thunder
> Snort in rampaging winds.
> Your feet are continually restless.
> Carrying your harp of sighs.

Published simultaneously with this eccentric yet wide-ranging selection is Ms. Hirshfield's third book of poems, a radiant and passionate collection called *The October Palace.* The two works share a heart: Ms. Hirshfield's interest in Buddhist teachings and mysticism insinuates itself as the link, becoming, in the words of one of her poems, "the breath-space held between any call / and its answer."

Thus, in this selection from the anthology the Persian Sufi poet Rabia offers a metaphor

> What is inside me, I don't let out;
> What is outside me, I don't let in. . . .
> I am a Doorkeeper of the Heart.

From a review of *Women in Praise of the Sacred: 13 Centuries of Spiritual Poetry by Women* edited by Jane Hirshfield; and *The October Palace: Poems* by Jane Hirshfield, in *New York Times Book Review,* July 3, 1994. Copyright © 1994 by The New York Times Co. Reprinted by Permission.

that segues neatly into a poem in Ms. Hirshfield's own collection, entitled "The Door":

> The rest-note,
> unwritten,
> hinged between worlds,
> that precedes change and allows it.

Nowadays, the attempt to discover women's political and historical identity through their literature has become an obsession. Little, however, has been done to document women's hidden lives, their spiritual leanings; nor is much written about women's religious communities, perhaps because the contemplative life thrives on privacy and resists definition. Yet some of our greatest female poets have been loners and mystics, from Sor Juana to Emily Dickinson.

As Ms. Hirshfield suggests, poetry is often prayer and prayer poetry. Though some of her excavation of the past is pure and fascinating religious history—as when she documents the writings of the Beguines, a northern European medieval lay order devoted to prayer and good works—the rest of the anthology is a choir of literary, religious, even royal voices. And so Saint Teresa of Avila is sandwiched between Maria de' Medici and the marvelous sixteenth-century Indian poet Mirabai.

The anthology's one flaw is a rather insistent reiteration of its theme, as if all women at all times wrote of oneness, the affirmative self and the awakened mind. Readers familiar with Dickinson's "loaded gun" or the darker passages of Anna Akhmatova (both women appear here as blissful avatars) will find the editing a bit biased.

Yet the reader cannot fail to hear the chord Ms. Hirshfield has struck as it reverberates from mind to mind, lyric to lyric, from Penny Jessye's deathbed spiritual to the Osage women's initiation song. Ms. Hirshfield's own beautiful verses take their place in this "found" tradition, which she has presented free of sectarian shrillness or the sword-and-gallows imagery of most conventional literary history.

Sons, Lovers, Immigrant Souls

The choice of Minnie Bruce Pratt's *Crime against Nature* as the 1989 Lamont Poetry Selection might have been viewed by some as a gratuitous egalitarian political choice. At last, a book by a lesbian mother. Who next?

This book is a publishing event, but not because of its radical or marginalized lesbian feminist viewpoint. It deserves attention because it is original, startling in the beauty of its unadorned voice. What authenticates the imagination here is a new and fearless eroticism and a refusal of received poetic ideas. Furthermore, Ms. Pratt's experience transforms itself into a pure "literary" obsession: the trauma of separation from her young sons after the breakup of her marriage flows out of *fact* into poetry, first as fixated grief then as a gradually evolving awareness that becomes a fearless moral stand.

Minnie Bruce Pratt is a natural lyric poet, but she shakes up her symmetrical music to accommodate the emotional power of her arguments. She is capable of familiar, elegant tonal beauty, even in indicting patriarchal poetry:

> When you were born, all the poets I knew
> were men, dads eloquent on their sleeping
> babes and the future: Coleridge at midnight,
> Yeats' prayer that his daughter lack opinions,
> his son be high and mighty, think and act.
> You've read the new father's loud eloquence,

fiery sparks written in a silent house
breathing with the mother's exhausted sleep.

Her situation as a mother separated from her children gener-
ates a rhetoric of extremity:

And here,
perhaps, you say: *That last word doesn't belong.*
Woman, mother: those can stay. Lesbian: no.

What inspires poetic emergency in Ms. Pratt's case is a history
of living outside the law (the "crime against nature" that pro-
vides the book's title is still specified in some state statutes). The
result of a life of "crime" is an imagination pushed to its limits.
The trauma, the suffering that inform these poems, make the
reader at once compassionate and admiring, for what has
sprung from this struggle is unfettered verse:

One night before I left I sat halfway down,
halfway up the stairs, as he reeled at the bottom,
    shouting *Choose, choose*. . . .
        There was no place to be
    simultaneous, or between. Above, the boys
        slept
    with nightlights as tiny consolations in the
        dark,
    like the flowers of starry campion, edge of
        the water.

This poem seems conspiratorial for all its directness—written
in code. What the husband is demanding is an absolute and there-
fore false division, a denial of the "in-between" where the mother
sits, torn between the freedom to live her own life and mother-
hood. We watch the poem deconstruct male power. He is, after
all, at the "bottom," not at the top, of the decision-making struc-
ture, where he perceives himself to be—and he is "reeling"—
even if he's being unreal. Ms. Pratt places heaven squarely on
earth, not at the bottom but in the all-surrounding sensual. The
flowers are "starry campion"; the children's nightlights are "tiny
consolations" (or constellations)—she is putting the world back
together, but in a courageous recodified female fashion.

Reading Their Signals

Jane Kenyon's new book, *The Boat of Quiet Hours,* seems more a condition of thought than a collection of separate poems. If she is indebted to Keats beyond her book's title—a paraphrase of a passage from "Endymion"—it is because she discovers, in the attitude of mind he called "negative capability" (a poet's acclimatization to states of doubt and mystery), her life. Sometimes this life is stiched plain as a sampler's koan:

> And I knew then
> that I would have to live, and go on
> living: what a sorrow it was; and still
> what sorrow burns
> but does not destroy my heart.

Sometimes she identifies, egoless, with the object of her contemplation—as when she writes that beavers in a nearby pool move "like thoughts / in an unconflicted mind." Nest building in the hoary reaches of negative capability offers further shelter for homeless thought—and a "longing" comes over her:

> It could be for beauty—
> I mean what Keats was panting after,
> for which I love and honor him;
> it could be for the promises of God;
> or for oblivion, *nada;* or some condition even more
> extreme, which I intuit, but can't quite name.

And the morning after oblivion: "I woke before dawn, still / in a body."

In "The Sandy Hole" Ms. Kenyon seems to hover above the tiny grave at an infant's funeral and provide, in the untouchable silence of the young father, a contemporary counterpoint to the brutal talk of the husband and wife in Frost's "Home Burial": *her* father stares at a coffin "no bigger than a flightbag" and is sealed in his grief, beyond human discourse.

These poems surprise beauty at every turn and capture truth at its familiar New England slant. Here, in Keats's terms, is a capable poet.

Patricia Dobler's *Talking to Strangers* is a kind of verse memoir about growing up in an Ohio steel mill town in the 1950s. Her immigrant Hungarian grandparents, parents and aunts and uncles—and the omnipotent, omnipresent steel mill—are all woven into the narrative tapestry. "Talking to strangers" is suspect, since "talk" itself is distrusted by these people, who have given up their old cherished tongue or hidden their use of it:

> Silence was the chosen one in whose deep lap
> you buried the Hunkie gutturals of sibilants,
> keeping back only the few consonants and vowels
> you thought your children would need in Ohio.

In most assimilation stories to succeed at being American is to fail to be one's true (traditional) self. Restated, it is exactly this failure of cultural identity that allows the transplanted generations to succeed at invention. Ms. Dobler plays on the tension between the generations—and the drama produced carries many of these poems. Whether it is the third-generation daughter writing verse or the father of the poet escaping from his family's "stories" to operate his ham radio at night, a new signal is broadcast into a future never imagined in the Old Country:

> Soon he will call "CQ" into the night,
> and a stranger will answer.
> "Do you read me? How's my signal?"

> Upstairs, I watch
> the herringbone pattern of his voice
> on the TV: my father, talking to strangers.

Line after line in this auspicious first book is lighted by the fire of the author's passion. If the rhetorical structures are sometimes setups, no one can argue with lines like:

> We laid the last course of firebrick
> in the big 3-storey kiln when something broke upstairs.
> Us brickies on the kiln bottom held our breath
> at the first whiff of lime, we knew that stuff
> could blind you, burn your lungs.
> Each man found another man's hand
> before shutting his eyes, so we inched out
> that way—like kids, eyes shut tight
> and holding hands.

And this passage from the powerful poem "Aphasia" is fresh from the same rhetorical caldron as Philip Levine's "They Feed They Lion":

> Because scared, because of *have to earn a dollar,*
> because for every thing you earned, Grandaddy sat
> on your shoulder saying "You're the lucky one,
> if you fell in the [toilet] you'd come up
> with a gold piece in your mouth," because traduced,
> laughed at, lied to, because you trusted only your hands
> and the perfect ribbons of steel rolling out of the mill.

That poem ends with the perfect elegy for the father and language itself. The meager acceptable "vowels and consonants" of the grandparents have evolved into this dark, flowering, meaningless tongue:

> because now you think "death"
> but say "black feather," here is a garden:
> pass your hand over the face of this thing you've forgotten,
> this "flower."

Marilyn Hacker's *Love, Death, and the Changing of the Seasons* has been called "a novel in sonnets" and a "verse novel" (à la George

Meredith's *Modern Love*), and, though the poems are as lyrical as they are narrative, the description is accurate enough. Faithful readers of Ms. Hacker's work will recognize names of some of the "regulars" in her cast of characters: Iva (Jr. and Sr.), Chip, Link, Karyn, Julie, Jax, Marie, and others. And a new name, Rachel, is added. The name is the heartbeat of this book, and in praise of the younger Rachel the poet gears up for one last spring:

> Well, damn, it's a relief to be a slut
> after such lengths of "Man delights not me,
> nor woman neither," that I honestly
> wondered if I'd outgrown it.

The poet (renamed The Hack) and Rachel (or Rae) begin a passionate affair that moves through seasons, real and metaphorical, like an express train. Most of these poems are sonnets (with a few villanelles and rondeaux thrown in). This armored form seems, as always, exquisitely suited to the lover's argument and to obsession. The poet's life certainly is obsessive, for, though she teaches, raises her daughter, shops at Bloomingdale's, travels to France, and eats four-star meals, her daily background is re-lighted, in relief, by the flame of her passion for Rachel.

Still, we are not stuck on one note here. Ms. Hacker knows how she sounds: there is irony inherent in her style. It is in her tone, her plot observations, even the poems' formal structures. She needs the "fix" of fixed forms. (It is further ironic that, when other lesbians and feminists avoid "traditional" architecture of "male" language as "written out" or "phallocentric," Ms. Hacker works grandly in the old "logical" forms.) She explains herself, faces the music, rewrites myths:

> Would we be heroes if things came to it?
> We only get to be tough guys in small ways,
> in Central Park, on highways or in hallways. . . .
> Achilles hung out in his tent and pouted
> until they made the *Iliad* about it.

And this one I love:

> ("What Does a Girl Do?"). What does a girl do
> but walk across the world, her kid in tow,

stopping at stations on the way, with friends
to tie her to the mast when she gets too
close to the edge? And when the voyage ends,
What does a girl do? Girl, that's up to you.

No one sings quite like this. A cappella, she's a whole choir.
elegant and versatile in the strictest forms, she is inventive and
exuberant in content. She's colloquial, lyrical, uncouth, old-
fashioned, and fun. (How many books of poems are fun?)
Here's an aubade to prove all that and display something much
closer to eloquence:

Five-thirty, little one, already light
outside. From Spanish Harlem, sun spills through
the seamless windows of my Gauloise blue
bedroom, where you're sleeping, with what freight
of dreams. Blue boat, blue boat. I'll navigate
and pilot, this dawn watch. There's someone who
is dying, darling, and that's always true
though skin on skin we would obliterate
the fact, and mouth on mouth alive have come
to something like the equilibrium
of a light skiff on not-quite-tidal waves.
And aren't we, when we are on dry land
(with shaky sea legs) walking hand in hand
(often enough) reading the lines on graves?

Passion, Politics, and Secret Rituals

On the acknowledgments page of Grace Paley's *New and Collected Poems* both the author and the publisher thank the person who "extracted" many of the poems from Ms. Paley's notebooks. This information is telling: the reader often feels like an eavesdropper on journal musings, personal and political anecdotes, speculative jottings. The book gives the impression of an album; one senses the poet "keeping track." Yet the poems do not represent any chronology; they float in the timelessness of old and recent snapshots. They offer themselves for us to browse through and exclaim over, to help us remember the dead, and the living moving toward death, the epigrammatic moments of personal history. They have the appealing amateurism of album snapshots: often a little out of focus, badly lighted, awkwardly posed. Still, they manage to hold our interest; they are funny and revelatory, with the occasional radiant economy of language that marks Ms. Paley's prose.

> the children are healthy
>   the children are rosy . . .
> they sleep without crying
>   they are very smart
> each day they grow
>   you would hardly know them.

From reviews of *New and Collected Poems* by Grace Paley and *Sub Rosa* by Susan Prospere, in *New York Times Book Review,* April 19, 1992. Copyright © 1992 by The New York Times Co. Reprinted by Permission.

The opening poems in the book have the feel of creation myths, retold from a woman's point of view, with revisionist metaphors:

> A woman invented fire and called it the wheel
> Was it because the sun is round
>   I saw the round sun bleeding to sky
> And fire rolls across the field
>   from forest to treetop
> It leaps like a bike with a wild boy riding it.

These "creation myths" expand to family stories and the poet's own experiences. At their best they carry the deadpan dazzle of Stevie Smith. "If I were in the middle of the Atlantic / drowning far from home," one begins,

> I would look up at the sky
> veil of my hiding life
> and say:
> goodbye.

At worst they're overly ingenuous, sentimental. Poems on dissent and political consciousness—some of them inspired by Ms. Paley's visits to El Salvador and Hanoi—are straightforward testimonies, and these are among the most powerful poems in the book. In them we recognize the Grace Paley we are most familiar with: the maternal, heroic and funny tough cookie— street fighter and storyteller par excellence.

In *Sub Rosa*, Susan Prospere's first book of poems, we are allowed into the privileged world of childhood. As the book's title indicates, these poems are "under the rose," operating under an ancient charm: the rite of hanging a rose, symbolizing the oath of secrecy, over the council table. The shadow of this rose, delicate, perfumed, hypnotic—both a seduction and a warning— darkens every poem here.

> In June there will be sweetheart roses
> along the whitewashed fences.
> Years ago I saw my father pin one on my mother

as if it were a corsage she would wear
to enter the evening.
Her body was limber then,
and the angels would have envied her had they seen her,
dancing in the Bahia grass a private dance
that did not include my father
or any of us who watched from an upstairs window.
This was the province of the sacred,
and we begged her with rising voices to come indoors.

We are effortlessly drawn into this world, so ordinary on the surface ("My brothers threw a baseball in the evenings in their bedroom— / the light outside, the color of Four Roses poured into glasses"), and then into the underworld, where secret rituals keep the world alive ("While we are sleeping, the adults go down / to the healing waters to recover their losses"). There are rites of cruelty ("Because you were the youngest, we told you / you were adopted"), and this cruelty has a terrifying beauty and symmetry. There is cruelty in family order, cruelty in children's language and isolation, each "select and sinful disposition."

Ms. Prospere's alchemy manages to turn diverse elements into gold. These poems are startling and transformational: an extraordinary debut.

"Go Be a King in a Field of Weeds"

Maxine Kumin sounds weary in *Nurture,* and with good reason. These poems are exhaustive in their sorrow: they are predominantly short, brutal elegies for the natural world. She recites, in bitter, gripping litanies, the roster of extinct life forms, along with those about to be extinct, and casts a cynical eye on humankind, the "unaware" species responsible for the destruction of the living world:

> With zoom lenses we look in,
>
> look in and wonder
> at what flesh does for them—
> we, who are going under.

Most of the poems are in understated rhyme, terse couplets, maximlike asides. The overall effect is one of anguished enumeration—as if the poet stood on the deck of a sinking Noah's ark, counting again each animal we are losing. This emotional census fails occasionally as poetry and becomes a kind of versified prose, with the characteristic lilt of a zoology text: but if we read these poems as exhortations in the plain style, if we read them to learn, they amaze, in just the way the naturalist's evidence amazes, because of their sheer wondrous detail. Of a trumpeter swan she writes:

> In the wild its head and neck are often rust-red
> from feeding in ferrous waters. There is

From reviews of *Nurture* by Maxine Kumin, and *Annonciade* by Elizabeth Spires, in *New York Times Book Review,* November 5, 1989. Copyright © 1989 by The New York Times Co. Reprinted by Permission.

a salmon or flesh-colored stripe, like a fine cord,
at the base of the bill. This is called the grin line.

Ms. Kumin's refusal of lyricism, a willed, pained abstinence in this late hour of the species, cannot muffle completely her home-grown music:

> Sleeping with animals,
> loving my animals too much,
> letting them run like a perfectly detached
> statement by Mozart through all the other lines
> of my life.

Refusing to see through the rosy glasses of a Rousseau, Ms. Kumin stays a realist. When a "she-leopard stalks and pounces on / an infant antelope," she asks: "which one / am I rooting for?" Both, it turns out, or neither—since, as she notes, the leopard's cubs are starving for meat. There is no easy sentimental solution. Nature is "a catchment of sorrows." The poems in *Nurture* triumph in maternal righteousness and strength, but Ms. Kumin also displays subtle wit and a talent for self-parody, catching herself in top form as "a lady with a lamp": "Bring me your fallen fledgling, your bummer lamb, / lead the abused, the starvelings, into my barn."

With her imagined adoption of the "wild child" of the famous nineteenth-century French case history, the whimsy is carried to the perfect extreme. Despite critics attacking her for an "overabundance of maternal genes," the narrator does not condescend to, pity or smother the wild creature with love. She finds a way to talk to wildness: "Laughter our first noun, and our long verb, howl." Ms. Kumin is tough-minded, succinct, compassionate: mother-protector, "a lady with a lamp." If poetry could save the world, *Nurture* would be the ark.

Elizabeth Spires's third book of poems, *Annonciade,* has a haunted feeling, but, unlike Michael Ryan's ghosts, hers seem firmly rooted in time and place. Each poem is placed carefully like a jewel in a setting. An occasional aura of "accomplishment" creeps in, the kind one associates with accomplished Victorian daughters spending long indolent afternoons at the spinet or doing hours of needlepoint and crewelwork. Her titles seem like sachets: "Fabergé's Egg," "Victoriana: Gold Mourning Pendant with an Eye Painted on Ivory," "The Comb and the Mirror," "Glass-Bottom Boat," "Puella Aeterna." Indeed, there are moments of literary window dressing here:

> O bitterly they tell,
> bitter to lose one of theirs,
> how moonlit nights you searched,
> moonstruck and bewitched,
> the caves of Pendour Cove
> for my flashing mermaid's mirror.

Still, Ms. Spires is too strong-willed and gifted a poet to succumb entirely to contrivance. Once past the brocaded curtains, we are in the presence of a circumspect and intriguing intelligence. Insights are bracing and often unexpected. In a poem about Josephine, a great Indian hornbill living in a park birdhouse, the poet draws a nutty solipsistic portrait:

> Her keepers exist because she exists.
> Quietly they pass, in green uniforms,
> each with a pale green grape for Josephine.

In "Victoriana: Gold Mourning Pendant with an Eye Painted on Ivory" she flies in the face of the title's ponderous setup and writes in short, furious syllabic lines, in an outraged contemporary voice:

> Who made this thing?
> An eye staring
> without blinking,
> laid down on the dead
>
> white of ivory.

"As if grief could be transformed / into a cold and costly object," she rages, and goes on, in stunning excoriation of the object, till she confronts death itself, fearlessly. This poem and others— like the hauntingly conceived "Profil Perdu"; the title poem, with its "Magic Mountain" eloquence; and "Woman on the

Dump," with images strikingly suggestive of the paintings of Edvard Munch—contain unforgettable writing.

The best poem in the book is "Sunday Afternoon at Fulham Palace"—for its delicate truce between beauty and horror, its utterly "natural" glimpse of nuclear destruction on a sunny afternoon: "The white peacock. Erased. The goldfish in the fountain / swimming crazily as the water boils up around them, evaporates."

Elizabeth Spires seems torn between love of perfection and love of passion: in this poem that delicate balance is struck.

Ourselves as History

A riddle of the ordinary is its mnemonic reality, its capacity for calling up the extraordinary response of memory. Conjure up Newtonian physics with the image of an apple, three generations of English royalty with a rhyme. We travel from the trivial to the metaphysical in one triggered synapse—and more significant than the success of acquired recall is the predisposition of language that facilitates recollection. The poet discussed here uses mnemonic devices in an expanded sense (hence metaphor, symbol) and writes with an understanding of this predisposition of the words and this same mystery of evocation and "recognition" on some other level of consciousness. Words are mnemonic, or symbols, in the most primitive sense; in poetry they are also *illuminators*: through chosen words memory retrieves not just the "answer" but the emotion, the intensity, the quickening hush of the recalled place or state of mind. In poetry time is irrelevant because the poet controls memory: the past can be delivered in a word. In the poem each word *is* a memory. Reading, we relive memories of others, of the poet; we start at recollections of things we have never known and suffer a sense of déjà vu so powerful that it leads us out of time, allows us to exist in the past and future simultaneously.

Lucille Clifton, in her third collection of poems, *An Ordinary Woman,* plays on this collective sense of déjà vu, by using the power of everyday objects. She records the riddle of the ordinary with deliberate irony. In the first poem in the book, "In Salem," the "black witches know" that terror is not in weird

---

From reviews of two books by Lucille Clifton: *An Ordinary Woman* and *Generations: A Memoir* in *Parnassus* (Spring–Summer 1976).

phases of the moon or the witches' broom or the "wild clock face":

> the terror is in the plain pink
> at the window
> and the hedges moral as fire
> and the plain face of the white woman watching us
> as she beats her ordinary bread.

This is an extraordinary "ordinary" poem, a homely and particular source of history, of memory, the bread rising as the witch burns and the sinister association made and given its full measure of terror and truth in the emphasis on *ordinary*—the word and the state of mind.

Wallace Stevens, in an essay on reality and the imagination, remarks that "the history of a figure of speech or the history of an idea . . . cannot be very different from the history of anything else." Thus "us" is "you and me; and yet not you and me as individuals but as representatives of a state of mind." (Adams, writing about Vico, and currently Michel Foucault echo this preoccupation with history as mental state.) Lucille Clifton seems bent on examining in this book the states of mind, the personal commentary, and paraphernalia that become momentous and historical. Her talent is for "news," facts that bloom into profundity or glamour, at best and worst, respectively. Her language has flex and determination. She is an *intensifier,* steeped in what Stevens termed the "lentor and solemnity" of commonplace objects. In "At Last We Killed the Roaches" all these elements come together to render a poem like a scream sealed in the walls, a family curse falling with the dead roaches:

> at last we killed the roaches
> mamma and me. she sprayed
> i swept the ceiling and they fell
> dying onto our shoulders, in our hair
> covering us with red. the tribe was broken,
> the cooking pots were ours again
> and we were glad, such cleanliness was grace
> when I was twelve. only for a few nights,
> and then not much, my dreams were blood

> my hands were blades and it was murder murder
> all over the place.

In one sense the mnemonic becomes moral. Cleanliness, instead of *reminding* us of godliness, *is* godliness. Clifton knows this distortion well: if "such cleanliness is grace," then the slaughter of the roaches becomes the bondage and slaughter of the black race—the "tribe was broken" and it was "murder."

Yet, despite this awareness, she occasionally, perversely, sets the same demon to work for her. The clock is thrown out the window, but we do not see time fly. It's just not enough, sometimes, the mnemonic: mentioning collard greens and Moses and Ms. Ann—although the words are touchstones and the phrases reverberate with the authority of common use (the ordinary), they remain strung out and glittering in air like a failed incantation. Lines like these unreel unashamedly:

> a love person
> from love people
> out of the Afrikan sun
> under the sign of Cancer.
> whoever see my midnight smile
> seeing star apple and
> mango from home.

This book is perhaps not ordinary *enough;* too much still stands in the way of our perception, too much bad romance and swagger in the self-consciously "black" poems as to render them almost gratuitous. We are not quite close enough to the real bone and tension of Lucille Clifton's individual life and imagination; we need to *feel* her life through the words, at points in consciousness and memory where they do not simply trigger set responses but function as they do in "In Salem": redefining the ordinary as new.

Just published and slight (a sort of footnote that got carried away with itself), *Generations: A Memoir* is not so much a memoir as a rocking-chair history, a tribute to a state of mind that survives. A case in point: "Get what you want, you from Dahomey women" goes the family maxim. The incidents recounted here, held together by a loose prose-poem mortar, swell with biblical intensity, tales of slavery and matriarchy: "Sister, we be strong women and weak men." Mammy Ca'line who walked from New Orleans to Virginia when she was eight-years-old. Lucy, the first black woman legally hanged in the state of Virginia (for killing the white man who wronged her). The author's father badgering Caroline for her African name ("or it'll be forgot!") and receiving her mixed admonishment and blessing, "Don't you worry, mister, don't you worry."

Like a séance, with a few raps on the genealogical table the ghosts walk. Like Mr. Sayles Lord, ladies' man and family man—"your crazy daddy," Clifton's mother would say—who could stop a dance by throwing down his hat. These prose-poems of evocation seem to me stronger in tone and fiercer in loyalty than the poems in *An Ordinary Woman*. Here there is testimony and legend—but no self-conscious attempt at "creating" black magic or the stage voice that sometimes preoccupies her other poems. The mystery and energy are already present in the words of these stories, told generation to generation. It is passed on, in the blood, in the narrative, don't you worry mister.

> Later I would ask my father for proof.
> Where are the records, Daddy? I would ask.
> The time may not be right and it may be just
> a family legend or something. Somebody somewhere
> knows, he would say. And I would be dissatisfied
> and fuss with Fred about fact and proof and
> history until he told me one day not to worry,
> that even the lies are true. In history, even
> the lies are true.

Amen.

Happiness, Death, and Jitters

In 1918 a pandemic called, variously, Flanders Fever, Spanish influenza, and the Contagion spread worldwide. By 1919 twenty-five million people had died, half a million in the United States alone. Ellen Bryant Voigt takes on this grim forgotten history in her new book of poems, *Kyrie,* an astonishing collection of sonnets so spare and tightly woven, yet so mindful of the cadences of the speaking voice, that the poems read like verse drama. Indeed, the dead (and the dying) speak with unconscious elegiac power, their stunned insights eerily apt for our own time, our own plague. At the book's end the voices of the dead rise, a Greek chorus, to accuse:

> Why did you have to go back, go back
> to that awful time, upstream, scavenging
> the human wreckage, what happened or what we did
> or failed to do? Why drag us back to the ditch?
> Have you no regard for oblivion?
>
> Don't you people have sufficient woe?

Why *did* Voigt "go back"? The poems are surely masterful, but the impulse to "capture" a time, to "re-create" the heartbreaking testimony of a ravaged community yoked by circumstance so powerfully to our time, would seem a rather obvious display of *Our Town* or Spoon River virtuosity. That *Kyrie* is not simply an exercise in topical imagining, that it is rather an illumination of

---

both tormented periods, is a tribute to Voigt's profound empathetic powers and to insights provided her by formal restraint.

Here is devastating illness against a backdrop of war—and not only the war but its breakdown of battle tradition with bombs, tommy guns, mustard gas, mechanized war machines. The old order dies, just as inexorably as the community unravels in the face of contagion. The two battlefronts are subtly juxtaposed.

> And so the armies could be done with war,
> and the soldiers trickled home to study peace.
> But the old gardens grew a tough new weed,
> and the old lives didn't fit as they had before,
> and where there'd been the dream, a stranger's face,
> and where there'd been the war, an empty sleeve.

And on the home front;

> How we survived: we locked the doors
> and let nobody in. Each night we sang.
> Ate only bread in a bowl of buttermilk.

Voigt examines here the contagious despair of modernity: the cynical isolation of the soul, the death of the community, the family, the estrangement of man from woman, of the *unlike* from the like-minded fearful and suspicious (once a congregation of thoughtfully religious souls, now a staggered mob of the afflicted).

> Oh yes I used to pray. I prayed for the baby,
> I prayed for my mortal soul as it contracted,
> I prayed a gun would happen into my hand.

That suicide gun stands as a symbol of the modern age—one of many details Voigt burns into the reader's consciousness. When the plague dead are laid out in the town gymnasium, there are many veterans in uniform among them: the ones "who'd been gassed, their buttons were tarnished green." Yet, again and again, she offers beauty. A brief brushstroke: a single jay in a bush is a "quick blue smudge in the laden spikes of lilac," like a messenger from another world.

She leaps from mind to mind, inhabiting each soul: letters from a soldier to "Mattie" waiting at home, soliloquies of the circuit-riding doctor, a schoolteacher who cannot comfort her feverish and crying pupils, an orphaned child, a child dying alone in an attic.

She has the historian's sure sense of conspiracy theory:

> It's simple enough arithmetic,
> so don't you think the Kaiser knew?
> Get one hog sick, you get them all.

Perhaps her most eloquent appraisal of our affliction—our acceptance of the *idea* that war is inevitable, that conflict among individuals is inevitable—is portrayed in the divided heart of the mother and the sisters, "complicitous":

> When does childhood end? Mothers
> sew a piece of money inside a sock,
> fathers unfold the map of the world, and boys
> go off to war—that's an end, whether they come back wrapped
>   in the flag
> or waving it.
> Sister and I were what they kissed goodbye,
> complicitous in the long dream left behind.

After the boy dies Voigt sketches in an "ending," a brutal, apt haiku:

> or the petals
> strewn on the grass, or the boys still on
>   the playground
> routing evil with their little sticks.

Kyrie makes the forgotten unforgettable. Here, the poet implies, is a germ of the alienated, angst-ridden holocaust thinking of the twentieth century, sweeping continents, ushering in the age of despair. If so many could die and so quickly—without the examination of history or theology, without the solace of a community, shoveled into mass graves and forgotten—we have precedent. Not only for magnitude of suffering but for our indifference to that suffering. It seems fit and just that these insights arrive in a book of poems, another forgotten medium of empathy, the kyrie of mercy. Voigt holds a mirror to the mouths of the dying and we see our own faces reflected.

Deborah Keenan has fearlessly titled her new book *Happiness,* no doubt aware that reactions to her choice will vary as much as interpretations of the H-word itself. What seems like a bold title to me could doubtless strike another reader as coy, ironic, self-indulgent or wise. Such an ambiguous little word. Once past the distractions of the title, the poems stretch out and breathe deeply, taking as long as they like. Happiness drifts in and out, masquerading briefly as joy, insight and, finally, lack of velocity—a slowness associated with summer, tropical sun, nursing—a lovely innocent deliberateness of the flesh. Slowing things down to recapture this state demands self-examinations—random histories of personal life, as well as histories of dreams, in which real domestic dramas unfold:

> My father asks if I remember his early beauty.
> He asks, "Are you happy?" but is gone before I can think
> of the answer he wants, the answer I have.

We never hear the poet's answer, and she invites us to speculate with her on the true content of contentment along with the daily dose of dread, the surge of skepticism and the sum of their effects on the soul. There is a very satisfying cumulative beauty earned by the poems' odd constructions: long looping lines of meditation, filling up the pages margin to margin like garden rows overgrown. The poems shuttle back and forth between past and present, craving a world that *coheres,* an end to suffering, guilt, betrayal—craving the peace and beauty of the maternal, while refusing every convention of that ideal.

> I wanted to stop the summer from leaving. I wanted to admit
> my complicity, the deals I make with work and sorrow, how I
> gamble for happiness every year, telling the devil or God

I'll be good or I'll be bad if I can just have that slowness
of summer one more time.

Yet there are also "maternal" poems of tenacity and fierce
tenderness that weave CNN reports of slaughter through panels
of sunlight falling on a nursing baby's face. Keenan posits mater-
nal love as an act of rebellion against universal rancor, though
most of her domestic poems are steeped in unabashed, passion-
ate doubt. These are, simply, poems about love (while not ex-
actly love poems) and the many forms it takes. They are finally
not about happiness. Best of all, they are smart enough to know
the difference.

In the Heart of the Heart of
the Country

Of poets who die young we sing passionate songs of elegiac praise; we lay the laurel gingerly on the grave, then step back weeping into the crowd of mourners. It is left to the critics, that flint-hearted lot, to moderate the pathos of the poet's departure, to warn against sentimentalizing the poems. Jane Kenyon, who died of leukemia in 1995 just after completing this collection of her new and selected poems, seemed to have found her own means to immunize her work against the condescensions of pity, the inflated language of eulogy.

The poems in *Otherwise* brook no sentimentality; their pathos is natural, apt. The poet here wears a housewife's apron, hangs wash on the line, walks a family dog and draws her thoughts from a melancholy, ecstatic soul as if from the common well, "where the fearful and rash alike must come for water." In ecstasy, she sees this world as a kind of threshold through which we enter God's wonder; in melancholy (she suffered from severe bouts of depression), the world is a stone oubliette, an airless root cellar.

Nothing escapes her attention. If a stone tumbles into her path, the stone grows luminous in her circumspect gaze. She has no truck with pathetic fallacy; where a lesser poet might overshadow the pebble with personal joy or grief, she demurs. The poems in this book, which include work from her first four collections as well as twenty new poems, are reflective, unswervingly focused on what we call everyday life, though, as she makes clear, there is no such thing as the ordinary. In reading these poems, we witness a kind of vanishing act—we watch the poet disappear into the point of contemplation, into the poem itself:

> The hen flings a single pebble aside
> with her yellow, reptilian foot.
> Never in eternity the same sound—
> a small stone falling on a red leaf.

Jane Kenyon claimed mortality—the transience, suffering and glory of living things—as her subject early on. Her attempts to handle this immensity were always instinctive, if not always sure-footed. She knew that the way to confront the universal was in the delineation of the particular—but her brushstrokes were broad at first, and she had to practice until she found a way to capture the eyelash flutter, the heartbeat, the white shudder of a window curtain. Looking at her earlier poems, we see an occasional propensity to wool-gather:

> All day in my imagination my body floated
> above the classroom, navigating easily
> between fluorescent shoals. . . . I was listening,
> floating, watching. . . . The others stayed below
> at their desks (I saw the crown of my own head
> bending over a book), and no one knew I was not
> where I seemed to be. . . .

This attempt at out-of-body travel pales in the presence of a poem from the same volume that prefigures her later, mature voice, speaking of the condition "which I can intuit, but can't quite name":

> I know you are thinking of the accident—
> of picking the slivered glass from his hair. . . .
> I wish you would look at the hay—
> the beautiful sane and solid bales of hay.

The poems often extol the restorative power of the land-scape, in particular the New Hampshire hayricks and meadows, the sight of the local farmers haying. In these poems, she is besotted with the idyll of the field, like the young Levin in "Anna Karenina"—although, like Levin, she is finally a romantic observer, not a participant. Haying becomes a perfect metaphor for her own split psyche:

> the soul's bliss
> and suffering are bound together
> like the grasses.

Despite the presence of strong New England influences, most obviously Dickinson and Frost (she writes in their plain style, with similar unadorned grace), Kenyon's vision of the countryside remains complicated by her sense of herself as observer, new neighbor. Though she is hardly an *arriviste* after twenty years, it is her husband's family whose names are carved on the gravestones in the churchyard; this is her adopted home. If Keats taught her anything, he appears to have taught her the perspective of transience, a feeling for how tiny and fleeting the poet appears in the landscape, yet how enormous the world's need for poetry, how universal its claims. When asked to write a poem in protest of the gulf war, she wrote the following:

> My old flannel nightgown, the elbows out,
> one shoulder torn. . . . Instead of putting it
> away with the clean wash, I cut it up
> for rags. . . .
> Making supper, I listen to news
> from the war, of torture where the air
> is black at noon with burning oil,
> and of a market in Baghdad, bombed
> by accident, where yesterday an old man
> carried in his basket a piece of fish
> wrapped in paper and tied with string,
> and three small hard green oranges.

The poem's absolute refusal to register the *I* of the ego or of protesting opinion (the same furious *I* whose avatar might start wars) fills it with uncanny compassion for all things. Even the flannel nightgown (once a soft, protecting shell of the self) becomes an *other,* and capable of pain. The implied question is inescapable: if we could see the enemy, the other-than-the-self, in such tender detail, how would war be possible? The poem, amazingly, is not sentimental; it is a little miracle of restraint and insight.

Other poems veer close to contrivedness, then transform themselves with the same miraculous touch:

> The dog has cleaned his bowl
> and his reward is a biscuit. . . .
>
> I can't bear that trusting face!
> He asks for bread, expects
> bread, and I in my power
> might have given him a stone.

Jane Kenyon spent the last twenty years of her life on Eagle Pond Farm in New Hampshire, the family home of her husband, the poet Donald Hall, who writes a moving afterword to the poems. Their marriage has been much celebrated (most notably in Bill Moyers's Emmy-winning special "A Life Together"), and though Mr. Hall is a familiar, affectionate presence, addressed as *you,* the poems settle finally into the floating temple of solitude.

It seems pointless to compare her to other poets, living or dead. (She has been hailed as an American Akhmatova, though her style differs significantly from that of the Russian poet.) Her words, with their quiet, rapt force, their pensiveness and wit, come to us from natural speech, from the Bible and hymns, from which she derived the singular psalmlike music that is hers alone:

> Let the fox go back to its sandy den.
> Let the wind die down. Let the shed
> go black inside. Let evening come.
>
> To the bottle in the ditch, to the scoop
> in the oats, to air in the lung
> let evening come.
>
> Let it come, as it will, and don't
> be afraid. God does not leave us
> comfortless, so let evening come.

Epilogue

How do we reassess the "subject-self," prevent it from consuming the objects in a poem? Boland lights up this process of re-envisioning objects when she examines Plath's poem "Balloons," (which appears on the surface to be a pretty, laconic poem about a tiny child puncturing a balloon.) But, (as Boland points out) without irony, the poem is "pre-erotic"; it occurs on a dangerous and shape-shifting sensory terrain. And Plath is not the familiar kamikaze-Medusa figure in the poem. She is a mother (though not the usual ironic casting of herself in that role) observing her children with love and clear-eyed prophecy, describing the balloons (party leftovers) floating free about the apartment as "soul animals." The poem is being written just a few days before her death by suicide. Her infant son grabs a balloon, peers through it into a transformed world—the world of unfamiliar color and imagery—then tries to *eat* this world (the reference to the mother's breast unavoidable), and the world he desires (naturally) explodes. Then he sits, a "red / Shred" in his fist, staring into "a world clear as water." The heartbreaking implication of the disappearing mother, of the privilege and danger of imagination, is inescapable, yet the poem is not shadowed by tragedy; it is a poem of blessing. Boland wants to disentangle the erotic from the sexualized, disentangle the sexualized from the feminist myth, and she does so here. She also gives us another sense of Plath. For a second she takes her out of the self in which we think we know her and gives her back her humanness. What she does, in essence, is to free her from the "truth," the loaded gun by which we have come to recognize her.

Page duBois says that women have not been allowed to *act* in narratives and that criticism has enforced this inaction. Further, women seem to long for a poem that is an "action." By sheer chance I ran across an article in *Modern Philology* that clearly establishes that women at the very intersection of the oral and written tradition accomplished both. I dislike the "biological inevitability" that pregnancy and birth metaphors carry for women, but one can look back on that silence following the oral epic tradition and find the following "metrics" apt.

Indeed, outside the epic tradition, far outside, where we imagine women and midwives conferred over kitchen fires, where women also moved house, fought for their lives, rode horseback; there were objects, shapes, even words, that functioned as active principles. The article in *Modern Philology* is entitled "Women's Medicine, Women's Magic" and examines Old English (Anglo-Saxon) metrical childbirth charms. Some of the charms are inscribed on parchment, cloth or wax, thus making the written text the material object. Some charms and prayers are directions on the page; these are meant to be said aloud and performed.

They *were* performed; each women spoke and acted these metrical charms in recognition of the presence of the child within her as a boundary within herself, the way the grave is a boundary between life and death. In one ritual the pregnant woman steps over her husband and speaks words: "Up I go, step over you / with a living child, not a dead one, / with a full-born one, not a doomed one." In another a woman who has given birth to a stillborn child takes earth from that child's grave, wraps this earth in black wool, and "sells" it to a merchant. The words she repeats accompany her action:

> ic hit bebicge   ge hit bebicgan,
> þas sweartan wulle   and þysse sorge corn.
> (I sell it, you buy it,
> this black wool and this sorrow's seed.)

Why does this dramatic action in language, why does the shape of a poem's journey within itself, argue beyond truth for its aesthetic inevitability? Perhaps because the abstract longs for a material manifestation like a soul for a body: for its object, action, shape?

There are many poems that make this point with visual and

sonic effects, sometimes in a single gesture. Witness Yeats's "The Second Coming" ("Turning and turning in the widening gyre"), Elizabeth Bishop's "In the Waiting Room" (the "ooooo" of Aunt Consuelo's cry of pain that becomes that black existential wave), Keats's extended hand, Dickinson's loaded gun.

But, again, I am biased. Poetic order is not predetermined, but shape may be. I am not a great believer in strict meter or rhyme or even accentual-syllabic rigor, but I believe in that "stepping over" a living body in the name of her unborn child. I believe in that woman grimly carrying a fistful of "bartering" dirt from the grave of her stillborn baby. The metrical charms, to my mind, represent the real beginning of the poem of the *act* of the woman poet's mind. As *any* poem becomes itself as an *act*, a motion of the mind.

I am pre-disposed to that truth about women. I was a child who walked around and around in circles, faster and faster, listening to music, telling myself stories. I enjoyed this benign fugue state for years. And long before that I'd learned how language can shape consciousness.

> I'm four, maybe five. In the backyard of our newly built house on Pascal Street in St. Paul, there is a new red swing hung over a stretch of sand. I'm on that swing, tentatively pumping as my mother pushes me higher and higher into the air. As she pushes me, she recites a poem by Robert Louis Stevenson, "How Would You Like to Go Up in a Swing?"
>
> What stays with me is not just the rather ordinary diction of the poem ("How would you like to go up in a swing? / Up in the air so blue?") but the shape created by the words, by the question-answer tension. I remember the momentum caused by my mother's pushes and how my own sensations become fear as she flings me from her into space, then exhilaration at *flying* outward ("Up in the air and over the wall / Till I can see so wide . . .."). Then, reaching a limit, I am pulled back into the field of the continuum.

I understood that poem viscerally, bodily. I felt it move in two directions at once. I was moving outward on the poetic line and returning at its end, I was *swinging inside the poem itself*, and I think my mother knew that. She knew that I would overcome my fear of leaving her and learn to love the poem all in one. Am I speculating here? Yes. I am hoping that there is truth in this: that one repetitive act embodied what she was both urging me toward and rescuing me from—a shape of a *self*, flying away. I was the little girl swinging within the ambivalence her imagination made for me, an endlessly fluid negotiation between woman and poet, poet and woman, my self and my source.